2nd Collector Steiff® Values

Complete Guide

American Limited Editions • Animal Kingdom

1980-1990

Disney® Steiff® — 1988-1995

Store Exclusives — 1980-1995

by Peter Consalvi, Sr.

Published by  Hobby House Press, Inc.
Grantsville, Maryland 21536

A Very Special Dedication...

To my daughter, Lisa DeMarco, for all the hours of time in assembling and inputting years of material.

A Special Thanks to...

Sheila Perry, Maryann DiIorio, Nadine Gravatt, and Constance Perry for the use of their bears in the beautiful photography. Also thanks to Constance Perry for the use of her house as a photography studio; Ben and Beth Savino for the Hobby Center Toys and Toy Store exclusive photos; and Dick Frantz for his vast Steiff knowledge.

Front Cover: (Left) Anniversary Limited Edition, Mother/Baby, 0155/38, LE 7500 pieces, 1981-1982, $600. **Frontispiece:** Margaret Strong, Captain Strong, 0156/34, LE, 1988-1989, $275. **Title Page:** The Walt Disney World Teddy Bear and Doll Convention Pieces 1988-1994. For complete listings see pages 32-37. **Back Cover:** Winnie the Pooh, 651243, LE 2500, Walt Disney World, 1994, $700. *Sheila Perry Collection.*

Photograph Credits:

Photographs of Steiff collectibles unless otherwise credited belong to the collections of Peter and Margaret Consalvi or Gary and Mary Ruddell. Photography by Tom Weigand Inc., Reading, Pennsylvania is featured on pages: 2, 7, 10, 15, 18, 22, 23, 27, 34, 47, 56, 58, 59, 62, 64, 70, 72, 73, 75, 77, 79, 85, 87, 90-93, 98, 102.

Photography by Michael Cadotte, Cumberland, Maryland is featured on pages: 3, 6, 7, 11, 14, 18, 19, 22, 26, 30, 31, 33-43, 46, 48-55, 57, 60, 61, 63, 65-68, 71, 74, 77, 80-83, 88, 89, 96, 98, 99, 102.

Additional copies of this book may be purchased at $19.95 (plus postage and handling) from

Hobby House Press, Inc.

1 Corporate Drive

Grantsville, Maryland 21536

1-800-554-1447

or from your favorite bookstore or dealer.

ISBN: 0-87588-447-4

TABLE OF CONTENTS

Unicorn, 0130/17, $160 and 0130/27, $195. Both LE 2000, 1983. *Sheila Perry Collection.*

WHY I DECIDED TO DO THIS PRICE GUIDE

As a salesman for the Reeves Company not only did I sell Margarete Steiff animals, but I also helped merchants with in-store Steiff promotions. At every promotion I was asked by collectors, "What is my discontinued Steiff worth?" Collectors also sent me long lists of Steiff animals wanting to know values for insurance purposes and for their own knowledge. Even merchants would call me seeking valuing information to answer questions posed by collectors. Indeed there are price guides, such as the *4th Teddy Bear and friends® Price Guide* by Linda Mullins and *Contemporary Teddy Bear Price Guide: Artists to Manufacturer* by Terry & Doris Michaud, which provide this type of information. Although these are excellent price guides, the books do not focus exclusively on Steiff made during the 1980s with the depth required to answer questions posed by the contemporary Steiff teddy bear and animal collector. My research, photographs and values are dedicated to the Steiff collector who loves the 1980-1995 era. Using my book, *Collector Steiff Values*, everyone can quickly identify when their animal was made, for how long it was produced, what the animal originally sold for, and its most recent collector value.

HOW TO USE THIS BOOK

First please read all introductory text so that you will know what collectors look for to identify, date and value their Steiff animals. I have undertaken this book, *Collector Steiff Values*, to make the user of the book an appraiser and to give them the data from which to identify, date, deduce important production information such as manufacturers suggested retail and the most recent collector value.

Organization of the Book

To aid the reader the book is divided into sections. The first section has the animals organized into type as many collect by their favorite animals. Each sectional listing has the data organized in numerical tag number order from smallest to largest. All animals produced by Steiff fall into one of the types: Teddy Bears, Disney, Steiff Collector's Club, Special Editions, Rabbits, Cats, Dogs, Farmyard Animals, Woodland Animals, Animals of the Wild, Characters or Steiff Specials (such as the Circus Wagons). A collector can see what they have in their collections and what they must need.

A separate alphabetical listing of all Steiff® Teddy Bears which includes the Disney, Collector's Club, Store Specials, and Steiff® Specials, begins on page 10.

Should the reader want a quick reference and has the tag number they can refer to the last pages of the book which has a listing of all the Steiff production sold in America plus Store Specials 1980 through 1995 and Steiff Collector Club specials, from the smallest tag number to the largest tag number.

How to Read an Entry from the Tables

Reading from left to right:

The Number corresponds to the number on the tag of the animal or set. The numbers after the slash refer to the metric size. The metric size measures the distance from either the bottom to the top of the animal or from the nose to the tail of the animal. The use of "00" signifies that this is a set of animals.

The Description may include the name of the animal; the description of the animal: including color, position of animal, whether part of a set, etc.; the abbreviations of LE means limited edition and mhr means made from mohair.

The Year and Amount Go across the entry until you come to the amount. This figure represents the suggested selling price to the consumer and reading up would tell the year of issue. Each ensuing price under each year would indicate the suggested selling price for that year. The last entry would signify that the animal was discontinued during that year by the manufacturer. Note: Because the book's coverage concludes with 1995, a price in the "current" column could indicate either an animal was introduced in 1995 with the suggested selling price or the animal was discontinued before a collectors value could be obtained.

Dino, 0050/28, LE 4000, 1990.

Giraffe St., 0759/15, 60" high, 1980-1987, 1989-1990, $2632.

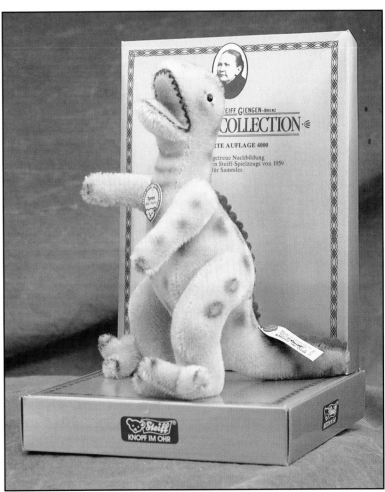

"Tyros" Tyrannosaur, 0051/20, LE, 1991, $250.

THE COLLECTIBLITY OF STEIFF®

Steiff has been making bears and other related animals for over one hundred years but it was the 1980s when Steiff would have their full impact on the American collecting world. Experts feel that this is due to the enthusiasm Steiff created with their 100th Anniversary Limited Edition *Papa Bear* (0153/43) released in 1980. Steiff had been creating playthings for 99 years when the unique event of how to celebrate the 100th anniversary of their first plaything dictated something special. The *Papa Bear* or 100th Anniversary Edition saw 11,000 created worldwide, 6,000 for Germany (with the certificate in German) and 5,000 for the United States (with the certificate in English). With this bear Steiff began a decade of releasing classic limited edition replica bears and animals (Museum Replicas or Editions).

Papa effected the public better than Steiff even expected. Dick Frantz, salesman for Steiff U.S.A. Ltd., was surprised at how well *Papa* was received. He knew that releasing a Steiff anniversary bear in the United States was a good venture, but he never thought it would have the impact that it did. *Papa* was ordered by retail stores and eagerly bought by collectors before he was even placed on the shelf. The next year Steiff released the *Mother and Baby* (0155/38) as part of the *Papa* series and the enthusiasm grew.

With the production of the *Papa Bear*, Steiff rekindled the general public's love for the Teddy Bear. *Papa* was produced with the same quality as the original and stuffed with excelsior. Excelsior was a popular stuffing material used by Steiff until 1972-1973. At this time some problems arose with the material. First, it was very difficult to work with because it required hand stuffing and took very strong men to perform the task. Then it also caused allergic reactions in some of the workers. It was abandoned as a stuffing because of those problems but Steiff reinitiated its use to produce the same quality bears as their early 1900s bears in 1980 and have been using it ever since.

The collectibility of Steiff is due largely to Steiff products being viewed as the ultimate in classic designs and depth of colors as well as to the quality and craftsmanship of their products. No company before Steiff has been able to produce replicas that are so similar to the original bears that there is absolutely no difference besides a little time. This is due to the time and energy Steiff takes to make an animal. Every piece of material is cut out by hand and sewn individually. The material is of the finest quality including mohair, trivara, and an incredibly soft Molly fabric used for children's toys. According to Cynthia Britnall of Cynthia's Country Store, "Each bear is a product of the best craftsmanship and material in the bear world. That is what makes them the best collectible on the market."

Steiff not only takes the time to perfect craftsmanship but they take the time to add realism to each piece with airbrushing techniques. This detail has separated them from any other plush company. The amount of airbrushing used on an animal varies. Sometimes it is used for shadow purposes and sometimes it is used for detail spots on a giraffe. Whatever the case, the airbrushing adds realistic detail to every creation.

During the 1980 decade, the demand for limited editions was high among collectors and the sales in this market skyrocketed. Specialty bear shops emerged to meet this demand, and Steiff animals and bears were available in antique shops, collector shops, toy stores, gift shops, doll shops, mail order, and appearing at collector shows throughout the United States. Steiff had a fantastic advertising strategy in 1980 that lead them to a great American market.

VALUE

The value of a Steiff collectible is determined in a variety of ways. The sophisticated collector is looking for a mint-in-box animal with all its tags, certificate, and original box. These items are often hard to find because not all animals have a certificate or special box.

Some of the important factors in determining a price are:

1. The color of the tag on the animal. There are two colors that are used — white and yellow. The white tag signifies a limited edition animal. These animals are more expensive and their current price and investment potential are determined by the number produced and demand by collectors.

The yellow tag means that Steiff has the right to reintroduce a line. An animal with a yellow tag is not limited to a certain number manufactured or timetable of production.

2. The number of pieces of an animal manufactured. This is usually determined by the color of the tag but that does not always hold true. Some yellow tag bears have become more popular and are in higher demand than some white tag bears. The most important distinguishing factor a collector is looking for is the color, the cut and the uniqueness of the bear.

3. Special Edition Bears. These include special editions made for stores like Mr. Vanilla of Hobby Center Toys and the bears made especially for the Walt Disney World® and Disneyland Teddy Bear conventions.

4. Condition. The mint condition animal has the original box, ear tag, chest tag, certificate, and occasionally the packaging carton. White tag bears were primarily boxed but some bears do not have a box. Boxed sets did not come with a certificate. In the early years of white tag manufacturing, the number of the edition was listed only on the certificate. Later this number was also placed on the ear tag.

GRADING

"Mint Condition" is the hightest grading any animal can receive. In order to have "mint condition", the animal must have all original tags, original box, and must be unsoiled. These bears are hardly ever removed from the box.

A piece may be graded "Excellent Condition" with no box, no breast tag, limited edition certificate missing, but generally in very clean, new condition.

Grading from this point on is "Very Good" slightly soiled, "Good" slightly worn, "Fair" soiled and worn, "Poor" soiled, badly worn and mold odor.

THE MUSEUM SERIES

In 1980 Steiff opened a museum in the first Steiff factory building in Giengen, Germany to celebrate 100 years of making playthings. This museum highlights every piece ever made by Steiff in a chronological presentation. It includes animals in mint condition as well as some animated displays.

The Museum Series produced in the 1980s are exact replicas of the earlier pieces. These pieces happen to consist mainly of other animals besides bears although some action bears (a bear on four wheels or a roly poly bear) are considered part of this series.

Museum pieces come in a silver box with no certificate and a numbered ear tag. They were not limited to a certain number in the beginning but were marked as a number but not marked as are limited editions out of the edition number. Limited edition numbers are now given.

Included in the Museum Series are larger pieces called studio pieces. These Studio pieces "Accomplish styling combined with the best materials and handicraft ability to produce large true-to-nature imitations of animals."

SPECIAL EDITIONS

This book would not be complete without information about special Steiff editions. These special editions are most interesting to collectors because of their limited distribution and scarcity as well as the unique influence such partnerships add to the Steiff design.

German Editions. From the first collector's edition, the *Papa Bear* has sprung others such as the 1988 *Teddy Baby and the Wolf* created for the Wolf Toy Store in Geingen. This unique

white *Teddy Baby* saw 1000 produced and its original sell-out offering at $200 has now increased in value to $650 on the collectors' market.

United Kingdom. Collectors also covet the usual 2000 to 3000 Teddy Bear editions produced for collectors in the British Isles. Harrod's, Hamley's, and Teddy Bears of Whitney (*Alfonzo*) have all produced special editions.

United States Special Editions. Suzanne Gibson Dolls made and distributed by Reeves International (who also distributed Steiff in the 1980s) also offered some special sets combining a Suzanne Gibson Doll with Steiff animals. *16" Suzanne Gibson Goldilocks* (#4003 from 1984-85) *with Three Steiff Bears* (25cm boy bear, 30cm mother bear, and 32cm father bear); *8" Suzanne Gibson Goldilocks* (#4004 from 1985-86) *with Three Steiff Bears* (14cm boy bear, 18cm mother bear, and 22cm father bear); and a *Suzanne Gibson Alice* (#4005 from 1986-1987), a limited edition of 3000 pieces, *with Steiff animals* (13cm cat, 13cm mouse, and 20cm Rabbit with big pocket watch).

1989 Ronald McDonald Dickie. 100 Dickie Bears were dressed in the Ronald McDonald Clown Outfits. They were sold to benefit the Ronald McDonald House.

WALT DISNEY CONVENTIONS

Walt Disney World and Disneyland Conventions have lead the boom in Teddy Bear collecting. These conventions, the first being in Walt Disney World, Orlando, Florida in 1988, highlighted specific artists and their bears. The Steiff bears produced for the Disney Conventions are much sought after by collectors for a variety of reasons. First, the very name Walt Disney conjures up excellence in design, creativity, and quality. Secondly, the Disney conventions set a standard of low numbered editions by the ultimate Teddy Bear manufacturer, Steiff.

Some special editions include the 1991 Walt Disney World® *Mickey Mouse bear*. This bear had a Mickey Mouse Masque and a Mickey head outline Steiff pin. The following year, 1992, a similar Minnie Mouse was produced.

Continuing the tradition of creating a likeness of a special Disney character, Steiff produced a *Teddy Donald* in 1993 and a classic *Winnie the Pooh* in 1994. This Steiff creation of Winnie brought new heights to the character collectibility.

The Disneyland conventions (1992 and 1993) had some pretty popular bears produced. Two of these bears have escalated quite dramatically in value as they are larger bears produced in small quantities. These bears came in two sizes and played music. The smaller bear played "When You Wish Upon a Star" while the larger bear played "When You Wish Upon a Star" and "It's a Small World After All."

TEDDY
BEARS

1909 Gold Teddies, 4-piece set, $0165/38, 1983, $358; 0165/28, 1984, $270; 0165/51, 1984, $587; 0165/60, 1985, $945.
Yellow tag. *Sheila Perry Collection.*

Previous Page: (Left) Anniversary L.E., Mother/Baby, 0155/38, 1981-1982, $600. (Right)
100th Anniversary L.E. Original Teddy, "Papa," 0153/43, 1980, $1000.

Steiff #	Description	1980-1981	1981-1982	1982-1983	1983-1984	1984-1985	1985-1986	1986	1987	1988	1989	1990	Current
0165/38	1909 Gold Teddy Bear, mhr, 1983 W				80	85	90	95				110	358
0165/51	1909 Gold Teddy, mhr, 1983 W					150	15959	169				435	587
0165/28	1909 Gold Teddy, mhr, 1983 W					55	59	62	62			75	270
0165/60	1909 Gold Teddy, mhr, 1984 W						275	290	290			580	945
0178/29	1938 Panda, mhr, LE					85	85					265	250
0178/35	1938 Panda, mhr, LE					110	110					320	350
0204/16	1982 The Teddy Tea Party, LE 10,000 U			175								300	675
0184/35	Alfonzo, Teddy Bears of Whitney, LE 5000, 1990 E												500
4005	Alice & Her Friends, (13cm Steiff Cat; 13cm Steiff Mouse; 20cm Steiff Rabbit w/big pocket watch), LE 3000,1986, Offered at $250 U												400
999765	Amelia, (with fliers coat/hat/goggles), I. Magnin, LE 650, 1993 U												600
406225	American Flag Bear 35cm, Polo, Ralph Lauren, NY, LE 3,500, 1992 U												425
0159/26	Antique Teddy Schwarz, J.P. Bear, Mary D's Dolls & Bears & Such, LE 1000, 1990 U												275
012013	Antique Teddy, Grey, 99cm DL, LE 1, 1992 U												N/P
11986	Antique Teddy, Grey, 30cm, DL, LE 1500, 1992 U												300
11993	Antique Teddy, Grey, 60cm, DL, LE 20, 1992 U												1500
12006	Antique Teddy, Grey, 80cm, DL, LE 1, 1992 U												N/P
0135/20	Baby Bear Pull Toy w/wagon, 1908 Rep, LE 4000 W										275	275	300
0225/27	Baby Ophelia witith Tutu, mhr, LE, 1988 U									140	140	140	200
0380/28	Baloo Bear	46	51									225	252
0218/16	Bear		28	28	28	28						60	67
6461/27	Bear (Hand Puppet)	26	28	28	28	28	28	30	36			60	67
6692/30	Bear (Hand Puppet)											85	95
6992/30	Bear (Hand Puppet)	46	50	51	51	51	51	54	65			85	95
650550	Bear Back Rider Set, LE 5000, 1991 U												300
0120/19	Bear Band Leader w/ Baton, LE									125	125	135	195
0120/19	Bear Band Leader, LE 5000, 1988 U												185
6370/22	Bear Music Box	49	54	54	54	54	54	54				97	109
0130/28	Bear on 4 Legs, Univ. Head Mov., mhr, LE 4000										400	400	550
0410/50	Bear on Wheels	200										685	1201
0085/12	Bear on Wheels, LE 12,000						95	100	100	120	120	165	175
0328/99	Bear Standing on 2 Legs								2963		4335	3895	4362
0128/33	Bear w/Snow White & Rose Red Set, Suzanne Gibson Doll Reeves International, 1987, LE 2000 U												400
1215/25	Bear, Lying											89	100
1212/25	Bear, Sitting											89	100
1210/25	Bear, Standing											81	91
0409/19	Bear, Standing St 69"	2493	2593									4700	5264
0201/10	Beige Teddy Bear, Jointed, mhr, LE					35	36					88	100
0201/14	Beige Teddy Bear, Jointed, mhr, LE				25	30	30					75	125
0251/34	Berlin Bear, mhr, LE, 1985 U					110	115	115				210	275
0173/40	Black Bear, 1907 Rep, LE 4000, 1988 W									300	300	600	800
0208/10	Black Teddy Bear, mhr, LE						36	38	38			88	119
0208/14	Black Teddy Bear, mhr, LE						30					75	125
0166/35	Blond Teddy, 1909, mhr, 1988 W									145	145	145	196
0166/43	Blond Teddy, 1909, mhr, 1988 W									225	225	225	304

Key: W = World Wide • U = USA • E = England • G = Germany • WDW = Walt Disney World • DL = Disneyland • N/P = No prices available

Steiff #	Description	1980-1981	1981-1982	1982-1983	1983-1984	1984-1985	1985-1986	1986	1987	1988	1989	1990	Current
0166/25	Blond Teddy, 1909, mhr, 1988 **W**									100	100	100	134
0155/36	Bride, LE 2000, 1984 **U**					100	110	125	150	200	200	215	300
0174/61	British Collectors Bear, LE 2000, 1989 **E**												800
0417/60	Brown Bear Cub		175	180	180							340	381
0329/16	Brown Bear Standing								2315			2500	3200
0329/08	Brown Bear Standing on 4 Legs								2315			2500	3200
1444/12	Browny Bear						23	24	30	50	50	32	36
1445/12	Browny Bear	17	20	21	23	29						42	47
0223/20	Bruno Bear, Jointed, mhr, LE **U**			60	60	62	62	62				135	250
0310/19	Buddha Bear, mhr				40	40	43					130	195
0293/32	California Musical Honey Bear, LE 2000, 1989 **U**												275
0156/34	Captain Strong Bear, 1987, LE **U**									200	200	215	275
0202/10	Caramel Teddy Bear, Jointed, mhr, LE					35	36					88	100
0202/14	Caramel Teddy Bear, Jointed, mhr, LE **U**				25	30	30					75	125
27079	Chairman II Bear 43, Polo, Ralph Lauren, NY, 1994, LE 1,500 **U**												800
0206/10	Chocolate Teddy Bear, Jointed, mhr, LE					35	36					88	119
0206/14	Chocolate Teddy Bear, Jointed, mhr, LE					30	30	30				75	125
0155/15	Christenening Bear, 1986, LE **U**							60	75	75		99	150
0156/32	Cinnamon Bear, mhr							69				135	350
0156/42	Cinnamon Bear, mhr, LE							100				195	450
0156/26	Cinnamon Bear, mhr, LE							53				100	250
0164/30	Circus Dolly Bear (Rare Pale Yellow) 1987 approx. 800 Pieces								135			245	375
0164/31	Circus Dolly Bear/ Yellow, mhr, LE 2000, white tag, 1987 **U**								135	175	175	185	250
0164/32	Circus Dolly Bear/Green, mhr, LE 2000, white tag, 1987 **U**								135	175	175	185	250
0164/34	Circus Dolly Bear/Violet, mhr, LE 2000, white tag, 1987 **U**								135	175	175	185	250
0100/90	Circus Wagon w/Two Bears, LE											450	475
0255/35	Clifford Berryman Bear, mhr, LE								170	225	225		300
0163/20	Clown Teddy, mhr, LE 5000										100	100	175
5352/33	Cosy Bear									110		110	123
5355/26	Cosy Bear		35	35	35	35	35	37	45			95	106
5355/36	Cosy Bear		55	55	55	55	55	58	70			95	106
5354/25	Cosy Bear, Dk. Brown			53	53							65	73
5353/25	Cosy Bear, Honey Gold			53	53							95	106
5358/18	Cosy Koala							45	55	80		80	90
5358/27	Cosy Koala			58	58	58	58					95	106
5358/28	Cosy Koala							70	85	125		125	140
5358/38	Cosy Koala							100	125			160	179
5358/50	Cosy Koala							200	250			320	358
5357/25	Cosy Panda					67	67	70	90	120		120	134
5405/17	Cosy Polar Bear					35	35	37	47	47		47	53
5405/30	Cosy Polar Bear				50	50	50	53	64	95	95	95	106
5505/25	Cuddly Bear			50	50							95	106
0172/32	Dicky "Clowns Around", Ronald McDonald House **U**												650
0172/17	Dicky Bear blond (for Circus wagon), LE 5000, 1990 **U**												130
0172/19	Dicky Bear Mauve, The Toy Store, LE 1000, 1991, (set) **U**												300
0172/18	Dicky Bear Rose, The Toy Store, LE 1000, 1991, (set) **U**												300
0172/32	Dicky Bear, 1930 Rep, LE 20,000, 1985 **W**						100	105	105	125		225	275
0217/34	Dorma Bear		65	66	66	66	66	70				145	162

Teddy Baby Brown, Replica 1930,
0175/35, $350 and 0175/42, $400.
Both LE, 1984-1990. *Sheila Perry
Collection.*

Margaret Strong Victorian Girl,
0155/34, $250 and Victorian Boy,
0155/35, $250. *Sheila Perry
Collection.*

"The Birthplace of the Teddy," 0162/00, L.E. 16,000 pieces, 1984-1987, $375.

Steiff #	Description	1980-1981	1981-1982	1982-1983	1983-1984	1984-1985	1985-1986	1986	1987	1988	1989	1990	Current
0215/35	Dormy Bear	60	67	68	68							150	168
5750/22	Drolly Bear											52	58
5600/18	Floppy Bear				36	36	36	38	48	65		65	73
5600/25	Floppy Bear				50	50	50					95	106
0155/22	Flower Bear-er, LE 2000, 1985 **U**						75	80	100	100		125	175
	Frau Nikolaus, Hobby Center Toys, LE 150, 1986 **U**												400
0218/14	Gieng-Ling Panda, Hobby Center Toys, LE 1000, 1988 **U**												400
0168/42	Giengen Bear, Blond, 1906 Rep, mhr, 1986 **U**							125	150	225		235	300
0168/22	Giengen Bear, Blond, 1906 Rep, mhr,1986 **U**							55	69	100	100	100	140
0167/32	Giengen Bear, Grey, 1906 Rep, mhr, 1985 **U**						85	90	100	160	160	160	225
0167/42	Giengen Bear, Grey, 1906 Rep, mhr, 1985 **U**						120	125	150	225	225	225	350
0167/22	Giengen Bear, Grey, 1906 Rep, mhr, 1986 **U**							55	69	100	100	100	150
0167/52	Giengen Bear, Grey, 1906 Rep, mhr, 1986 **U**							195	250	350	350	350	140
0167/26	Giengen Teddy Bear Grey, 1906 Rep, 1985 **U**												185
0168/32	Giengen Teddy Bear, Blond, 1988 **W"**												225
0162/00	Giengen Teddy Set, "The Birthplace of the Teddy," LE 1600, 1984 **W**					150	159	159	159			260	375
0243/32	Gold Bear w/Red Ribbon, mhr, WDW, LE 1000, only 500 produced, 1988 **U**									95			750
8501/02	Gold Plated Bar Pin w/Jointed Bear							15	18	27		22	25
8505/01	Gold Plated Teddy Earrings						20	21	27	46	46	46	52
8510/02	Gold Plated Teddy Necklace					15	15	16	20	32	32	210	33
0285/29	Golden Gate Bear, FAO Schwarz/San Francisco, LE 2000, 1989 **U**												600
0173/14	Goldilock Bear Boy (part of set #4004), LE, 1985 **U**												150
0173/22	Goldilock Bear Boy (part of set #4004), LE, 1985 **U**												175
0173/25	Goldilock Bear Father, (part of set #4004), LE, 1985 **U**												200
0173/18	Goldilock Bear Mother (part of set #4004), LE												200
0173/30	Goldilock Bear Mother, (part of set #4003), LE, 1984 **U**												250
4003	Goldilocks 16" & 3 Steiff Bears, Reeves International, (0173/25, Boy; 0173/30, Mother; 0173/32, Father),1984,Offered at $200 **U**												750
4004	Goldilocks 8" & 3 Steiff Bears, Reeves International, 0173/25. Boy; 0173/18, Mother; 0173/22 Father), 1985, Offered at $200 **U**												450
0173/32	Goldilocks Bear, Father (part of set #4003), LE, 1984 **U**												275
651861	Golli G & Teddi B, The Toy Store, LE 1500, 1995 **U**												400
0207/10	Grey Teddy Bear, mhr, LE						36	38	38			88	119
0207/14	Grey Teddy Bear, mhr, LE						30					75	101
0155/37	Groom, LE 2000, 1984 **U**					100	110	125	150	200	200	215	300
0226/28	Growling Bear											100	135
0228/33	Growling Bear, mhr								90	125	125	125	169
0228/38	Growling Bear, mhr								125	165	165	165	223
0228/48	Growling Bear, mhr								195	250	250	250	338
0181/36	Hamleys Bear Oliver, LE 2000, 1990 **E**												N/P
0163/26	Hamleys Bear, LE 2000, 1988 **E**												350
0168/28	Hamleys Bear, LE 2000, 1989 **E**												250
0296/38	Hamleys Tobias mit musikwerk, LE 2000, 1992 **E**												350

TEDDY BEARS – ALPHABETICAL

Steiff #	Description	1980-1981	1981-1982	1982-1983	1983-1984	1984-1985	1985-1986	1986	1987	1988	1989	1990	Current
0201/14	Hans Helfer, Hobby Center Toys, LE 200, 1987 U												250
0277/28	Hans, Marshall Fields, 1985 U												300
0169/65	Happy Anniversary, 1926 Rep, LE 5000, 1990 U											525	1100
6485/32	Happy Bear										95	95	106
0151/27	Harrods Musical Bear 1904/05, LE 2000, 1990 E												395
650680	Harrods Musical Bear 1906, LE 2000, 1993 U												400
0291/26	Harrods Musical Bear 1909, LE 2000, 1989 E												375
0294/42	Harrods Musical Bear 1920, Elise von Beethoven, LE 2000, 1991 E												N/P
0278/28	Helga, Marshall Fields, 1985 U												300
0260/25	Jackie Bear Rose, Doll House Southern Bear, LE 1000, 1990 U												273
0190/25	Jackie Bear, 1953 Rep, mhr, LE 10,000, 1987 W							110	135			295	275
0190/17	Jackie Bear, 1953 Rep, mhr, LE 12,000 W										135	135	175
0190/35	Jackie Bear, 1953 Rep, mhr, LE 4000, 1988 U									300	300	300	350
2877/30	Jr. Petsy			74	74	74						130	146
5701/22	Kiddi Bear										75	75	84
5702/20	Kiddi Bear										75	75	84
0140/38	Klein Archie, Enchanted Dollhouse, LE 2500 U												175
1446/11	Koala Bear	22	23	23	23	23	25	30	42	42	42	45	50
0160/00	M. Strong Choc. Brown Set, 4pc. LE 2000 U			275								480	850
0156/37	M. Strong Victorian Gentleman, LE, 1987 U							150	150	150		195	250
0156/36	M. Strong Victorian Lady, LE, 1987 U							150	150	150		195	250
0155/38	Mama & Baby, mhr, LE 8000, 7500 U		150									495	600
0245/32	Margaret Strong Bear, Grey mhr, WDW, LE 1000, 1990 U											125	400
0155/42	Margaret Strong Bear, mhr, LE, 1983 U				90	95	100	105	125	200	200	200	240
0155/26	Margaret Strong Bear, mhr, LE, 1984 U		48	48	50	53	56	69		100	100	100	120
0155/32	Margaret Strong Bear, mhr, LE, 1984 U		62	62	65	69	73	89		135	135	135	160
0245/80	Margaret Strong Bear, WDW, LE 1, 1989 U												N/P
0156/00	Margaret Strong Cinnamon Bear Set, mhr, LE 2000, 1984 U					300	300					590	900
0157/42	Margaret Strong Cream Bear, mhr, LE, 1984 U					95	100	105				265	450
0157/26	Margaret Strong Cream Bear, mhr, LE, 1984 U					50	53	56				145	250
0157/32	Margaret Strong Cream Bear, mhr, LE, 1984 U					65	69	73				185	350
0157/51	Margaret Strong Cream Bear, mhr, LE, 1985 U						195	205				565	700
0157/60	Margaret Strong Cream Bear, mhr, LE, 1985 U						285	300				625	1200
0155/51	Margaret Strong Gold Bear, mhr, LE, 1983 U					185	195	205	250	350	350	350	360
0155/60	Margaret Strong Gold Bear, mhr, LE, 1984 U					250	285	300	375	495	495	495	425
0158/41	Margaret Strong White Bear, Leather Paws, mhr, LE 2000 U							110	110	110		325	1000
0158/31	Margaret Strong White Bear, Leather Paws, mhr, LE 2500 U							79	79	79		255	600
0158/25	Margaret Strong White Bear, Leather Paws, mhr, LE 3000 U							60	60	60		165	400
0158/50	Margaret Strong White Bear, Leather Paws, mhr, LE 750 U								225			1200	1600
0245/60	Margaret Strong Bear, WDW, LE 10, 1989 U												N/P
600393	Martini Bear, Polo, Ralph Lauren, NY, 1994, LE 1500 U												800
0246/32	Mickey Bear, 32 cm, WDW, LE 1500, 1991 U												650
0246/80	Mickey Bear, WDW, LE 1, 1991 U												N/P
0246/99	Mickey Bear, WDW, LE 1, 1991 U												N/P
0246/60	Mickey Bear, WDW, LE 20, 1991 U												3000

Sailor Girl, 0281/28, 1986, $196. *Sheila Perry Collection.*

Museum Editions.
Left: Felt Elephant, Replica 1880, 0080/08, LE, 1984-1989, $101.
Middle: Roly Poly Bear, 1894 Replica, 0082/20,
LE, 1984-1989, $150.
Right: Bear on Wheels, 0085/12, LE, 12,000, 1985-1989. $175.

Soft Mohair Bears, yellow tags. *Sheila Perry Collection.*

Muzzle Bears, 0174/60, $700; 0174/46, $450; 406126; 0174/35, $270. All LE, 1988. *Nadine Gravatt Collection.*

Steiff #	Description	1980-1981	1981-1982	1982-1983	1983-1984	1984-1985	1985-1986	1986	1987	1988	1989	1990	Current
3490/45	Mimic Bear				75	75	75	79	95			165	185
5652/16	Min Floppy Polar Bear										50	50	56
5651/16	Mini Floppy Bear										50	50	56
0312/30	Minky Zotty									135	135	89	100
0312/40	Minky Zotty									200	200	130	151
0312/50	Minky Zotty									250	250	155	174
011870	Minnie Bear, 60cm, WDW, LE 20, 1992 U												2200
11863	Minnie Bear, 80cm, WDW, LE 1, 1992 U												N/P
11863	Minnie Bear, 99cm, WDW, LE 1, 1992 U												N/P
11863	Minnie Bear, WDW, LE 1500, 1992 U												650
1232/25	Mohair Soft Schwarzbear (Black Bear Cup), FAO Schwarz, LE 2000, 1990 U												250
0330/32	Molly Bear	36	40	41	41	45	45	48	58	95	95	95	106
0330/45	Molly Bear	84	97	100	100	100	100	105	125	160		175	196
0330/70	Molly Bear	190	250	265	265	265						410	459
0343/25	Molly Bear										150	97	109
0343/32	Molly Bear										220	145	498
0343/40	Molly Bear										325	205	230
0345/35	Molly Bear										205	135	151
0345/45	Molly Bear										290	185	207
0345/60	Molly Bear										350	230	258
0345/80	Molly Bear										575	375	420
0347/55	Molly Bear, Brown											165	185
0331/33	Molly Bear, Sitting									185	185	185	207
0333/35	Molly Grizzly		95	98	98							180	202
0331/22	Molly Koala	37	40									76	85
0331/40	Molly Koala	68	68									125	140
0318/42	Molly Minky									160	160		179
	Molly Minky										115	77	86
0323/65	Molly Panda		158	165	165							295	330
0326/32	Molly Panda, B/W	52	58	60	60	60	60	65	78	110	110	110	123
0326/45	Molly Panda, B/W	93	100	110	110	110	110	115	140	190		190	213
0327/32	Molly Panda, Brown	48	54									130	146
0327/45	Molly Panda, Brown	90	100									220	246
0332/45	Molly Petsy		95	98	98	98						180	202
0334/45	Molly Polar Bear		95	98	98							180	202
0334/55	Molly Polar Bear		140	145								270	302
0355/35	Molly Polar Bear, Sitting											135	151
0320/55	Molly Teddy		115	120								230	258
0320/65	Molly Teddy		160	165	165	165	165	175	210	265	265	165	200
0324/75	Molly Teddy											265	297
0323/60	Molly Teddy, Brown											175	196
0321/22	Molly Teddy, Champagne									65	65	42	47
0321/32	Molly Teddy, Champagne									115	115	70	78
0321/55	Molly Teddy, Champagne				100	100	100	105	140	200	200	125	140
0322/22	Molly Teddy, Cream									65	65	42	47
0322/32	Molly Teddy, Cream									115	115	70	78
0322/40	Molly Teddy, Cream					80	80	85	110	150	150	96	108
0151/25	Mr. Cinnamon Bear, (1904), LE, 1984 U					70	75	79				165	275
0151/32	Mr. Cinnamon Bear, (1904), LE, 1984 U					85	90	95				265	350
0151/40	Mr. Cinnamon Bear, (1904), LE, 1984 U					125	135	145				435	450
0151/55	Mr. Cinnamon Bear, (1904), LE, 1985 U												500
0151/26	Mr. Cinnamon Bear, 1984 U												275
0152/25	Mr. Vanilla, Hobby Center Toys, LE 1000, 1989 U												475

Key: W = World Wide • U = USA • E = England • G = Germany • WDW = Walt Disney World • DL = Disneyland • N/P = No prices available

TEDDY BEARS – ALPHABETICAL

Steiff #	Description	1980-1981	1981-1982	1982-1983	1983-1984	1984-1985	1985-1986	1986	1987	1988	1989	1990	Current
652080	Musikteddy 33, FAO Schwarz, LE 2000, 1993 U												350
0174/35	Muzzle Bear, White, 1908 Rep, LE 6000, 1990 U											295	270
0174/60	Muzzle Bear, White, 1908 Rep, mhr, LE 2650, 1989 U										500	500	700
0174/46	Muzzle Bear, White, 1908 Rep, mhr, LE 5000, 1989 U									375	375	375	450
	Nicholaus Bar, Hobby Center Toys, LE 300, 1985 U												450
8455/22	Nimrod Bear, Brass, Broken Set, LE					45						100	135
8452/22	Nimrod Bear, Caramel, Broken Set, LE					45						100	135
8453/22	Nimrod Bear, White, Broken Set, LE					45	35					96	135
0210/22	Nimrod Teddy Set, Teddy Roosevelt Comm. Set, mhr, LE 10,000 U				1100							275	550
0225/42	Ophelia Bear, Jointed, mhr, LE, 1984 U					150	159	169	1100	275	275	275	395
650918	Original Teddy Bar 36, Spielzeug Ring, Baumwollsack, Germany, LE 3000 W												N/P
0207/36	Original							62	62	115	115	115	201
0201/99	Original Bear Beige, mhr			700	700	750	795	850	9100	1450		2300	3000
420047	Original Steiff Teddybar 1908 Steiff Aug 1994 Worldwide Steiff Club												400
0201/41	Original Teddy Bear, Beige, mhr			70	75	75	79	85	100	160	160	160	275
0201/51	Original Teddy Bear, Beige, mhr			115	120	120	125	135	165	250	250	250	350
0201/75	Original Teddy Bear, Beige, mhr				450	500	529	560	675	975	975	975	1300
0203/11	Original Teddy Bear, White, mhr			13	15	19	20	21	25			39	80
0203/26	Original Teddy Bear, White, mhr			33	36	40	43	45	55			110	192
0203/36	Original Teddy Bear, White, mhr			48	50	55	59	62	75			175	306
0203/41	Original Teddy Bear, White, mhr			70	75	75	79	85	100			235	411
0203/51	Original Teddy Bear, White, mhr				120	120	125	135	165			310	543
0203/75	Original Teddy Bear, White, mhr				450	500						1250	1688
0203/99	Original Teddy Bear, White, mhr				700	750						2800	3780
0203/18	Original Teddy White, mhr				30	35	37	39	47			87	152
0201/11	Original Teddy, Beige, mhr	9	10	13	15	19	20	21	25	30	30	30	70
0201/18	Original Teddy, Beige, mhr				30	35	37	39	47	70	70	70	125
0201/26	Original Teddy, Beige, mhr	27	30	33	36	40	43	45	55	85	85	85	150
0201/36	Original Teddy, Beige, mhr	36	40	48	50	55	59	62	75	115	115	115	225
0209/12	Original Teddy, Black, mhr											50	67
0209/15	Original Teddy, Black, mhr											70	125
0210/12	Original Teddy, Blond, Mini-Mohair										50	50	67
0210/15	Original Teddy, Blond, Mini-Mohair										70	70	125
0205/26	Original Teddy, Caramel	32	35	37	37	45	45	48	58			80	108
0205/35	Original Teddy, Caramel	45	50	52	54	62	62	66	80			110	149
0205/50	Original Teddy, Caramel	97	105	120	120	120						235	317
0202/11	Original Teddy, Caramel, mhr	9	10	13	15	19	20	21	25	30	30	30	70
0202/18	Original Teddy, Caramel, mhr				30	35	37	39	47	70	70	70	125
0202/26	Original Teddy, Caramel, mhr	27	30	33	36	40	43	45	55	85	85	85	150
0202/36	Original Teddy, Caramel, mhr	36	40	48	50	55	59	62	75	115	115	115	225
0202/41	Original Teddy, Caramel, mhr	53	60	70	75	75	79	85	100	160	160	160	275
0202/51	Original Teddy, Caramel, mhr	84	100	115	120	120	125	135	165	250	250	250	350
0202/75	Original Teddy, Caramel, mhr				450	500	529	560	675	975		1195	1300
0202/99	Original Teddy, Caramel, mhr				700	750	795	850	9100	1450		2300	3105
0202/12	Original Teddy, Caramel, Mini-Mohair										50	50	70
0202/15	Original Teddy, Caramel, Mini-Mohair										70	70	100
0206/11	Original Teddy, Choc. Brown, mhr					19	20	21	25	30	30	30	65
0206/18	Original Teddy, Chocolate Brown, mhr					35	37	39	47	70	70	70	123
0206/26	Original Teddy, Chocolate Brown, mhr					40	43	45	55	85	85	85	149

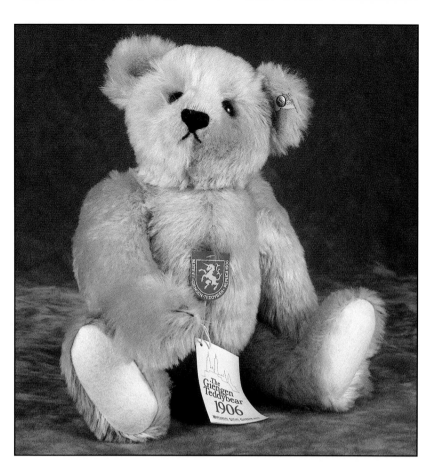

Grey Giengen, yellow tag, #0167/42, 1985, $550.
Sheila Perry Collection.

Circus Dolly Bear, LE 2000, white tag, 1987-1989.
(Left) Yellow, 31cm, 0164/31, $250;
(Center) Violet, 34cm, 0164/34, $250.
(Right) Green, 32cm 0164/32, $250.

Margaret Woodbury Strong Chocolate Brown Set, 4 pieces, 0160/00, $850, LE 2000, 1983-1984. (Left) 0160/32. (Right) 0160/42.

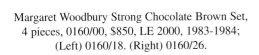

Margaret Woodbury Strong Chocolate Brown Set, 4 pieces, 0160/00, $850, LE 2000, 1983-1984; (Left) 0160/18. (Right) 0160/26.

Steiff #	Description	1980-1981	1981-1982	1982-1983	1983-1984	1984-1985	1985-1986	1986	1987	1988	1989	1990	Current
0206/36	Original Teddy, Chocolate Brown, mhr					55	59	62	75	115	115	115	201
0206/41	Original Teddy, Chocolate Brown, mhr					75	79	85	100	160	160	160	280
0206/51	Original Teddy, Chocolate Brown, mhr					120	125	135	165	250	250	250	438
0213/10	Original Teddy, Cinnamon, mhr, LE							38	38			82	111
0212/10	Original Teddy, Cream, mhr, LE							38	38			82	111
0214/10	Original Teddy, Gold, mhr, LE							38	38			82	111
0207/12	Original Teddy, Grey, mhr											50	67
0207/15	Original Teddy, Grey, mhr											70	94
0207/26	Original Teddy, Grey, mhr, LE							45	45	85	85	85	149
0207/41	Original Teddy, Grey, mhr, LE							85	85	160	160	160	280
0211/10	Original Teddy, Rose, LE 8000											60	81
0211/12	Original Teddy, Rose, mhr											50	67
0211/15	Original Teddy, Rose, mhr											70	94
0220/30	Orsi Bear	48	54	55	55							120	150
0439/07	Panda					150							600
0439/13	Panda					425							1300
0477/60	Panda Bear Cub		188	195	195							345	386
0153/43	Papa Bar, 100th Annv, LE 5,000, Original Teddy **U**	150										800	1000
0245/40	Passport Bear, mhr, LE, 1985 **W**						110	115	140	210		225	304
51847	Petsil, The Toy Store, LE, 1500, 1993 **U**												175
651847	Petsile, The Toy Store, LE 1000, 1993 **U**												195
0180/50	Petsy Bear, Ctr. Seam Bicolor, mhr, LE 5000, 1989/90 **U**										375	375	700
0181/35	Petsy Bear, Rep Ctr Seam Brass, mhr, LE 5000 **W**										225	225	395
0244/35	Petsy Bear, White, WDW, LE, 1000, 1989 **U**										115		500
0240/28	Petsy Panda							60	72	110	110	68	76
0240/35	Petsy Panda							80	96	150	150	150	168
0240/45	Petsy Panda							115	140	200		200	224
0224/35	Petsy Soft											93	104
0238/35	Petsy Teddy											85	95
0236/28	Petsy Teddy, Augbergine											62	69
0237/28	Petsy Teddy, Blackberry											62	140
0245/80	Petsy, 80cm, WDW, LE 1, 1990 **U**												N/P
0245/99	Petsy, 99cm, WDW, LE 1, 1990 **U**												N/P
7492/05	Pitty Bear	6	7									15	17
0470/99	Polar Bear			2565	2565							4600	5152
0472/99	Polar Bear			945	945	945	945	1195			1843	1700	1904
1447/17	Polar Bear		25	26	26							50	56
0468/60	Polar Bear Cub		175	180	180							340	381
0090/11	Polar Bear Jntd Legs/Rtng Head, LE 3000								95	95	155		200
1225/25	Polar Bear, Lying										89		100
1222/25	Polar Bear, Sitting										89		100
1220/25	Polar Bear, Standing										81		91
0467/23	Polar Bear, White	50	57	58							95		106
0166/32	Preppy Bear 35, Polo, Ralph Lauren, NY, 1991/92 **U**												350
027062	Preppy Bear 35, Polo, Ralph Lauren, NY, 1994 **U**												350
27093	Producer Bear 43, Polo, Ralph Lauren, NY,1994, LE 1500 **U**												800
5030/17	Pummy Bear										90	90	101
5030/21	Pummy Bear										115	115	129
5035/17	Pummy Koala Bear										105	105	118
5035/21	Pummy Koala Bear										140	80	90
0116/25	Record Teddy, 1913, LE 4000, 1990 **W**											300	350

Teddy Bears – Alphabetical

Steiff #	Description	1980-1981	1981-1982	1982-1983	1983-1984	1984-1985	1985-1986	1986	1987	1988	1989	1990	Current
0150/32	Richard Steiff 1902-1903 Bear, LE 20,000 **W**				90	100						285	400
8155/50	Riding Animal, Bear on Wheels		285	290	295							565	632
8150/40	Riding Animal, Riding Bear Rocker		205	210	215	285	285	300				395	442
8130/50	Riding Animal, Rocking Bear			285	295	295	295	310	375	600	600	385	600
8010/40	Riding Bear	185										355	398
0155/23	Ring Bear-er, LE 2000 pc. 1985 **U**						75	80	100	100		125	175
0115/18	Roly Poly Bear w/Rattle 1908, mhr, LE								125	125	125		145
0155/18	Roly Poly Bear with rattle, 1908 Rep, 1990 **U**												150
0082/20	Roly Poly Bear, 1894, 2 yr LE						69	70	70	80	80	95	150
0131/00	Rub-A-Dub-Dub Set, 3 Bears in a Tub, LE 2000, 1988 **U**								275	275		310	350
0131/24	Rub-A-Dub-Dub Set, brass, Candlemaker, LE 2000, 1988 **U**												140
0131/25	Rub-A-Dub-Dub Set, brown butcher, LE 2000, 1988 **U**												140
0131/23	Rub-A-Dub-Dub Set, yellow, Baker, LE 2000 **U**												140
650581	Russia Bear, Polo, Ralph Lauren, NY, 1994, LE 1500 **U**												350
0237/20	S-Soft Teddy, Beige, Jointed, mhr, LE					40						90	101
0237/28	S-Soft Teddy, Beige, Jointed, mhr, LE					55	59	62	62			125	140
0237/35	S-Soft Teddy, Beige, Jointed, mhr, LE					75	79	85	85			165	185
0237/45	S-Soft Teddy, Beige, Jointed, mhr, LE					110	115	115	115			245	274
420801	Sam 28, Steiff Club, LE 4000, 1993/94 **U**												750
0155/38	Santa Bear, 1000 pc., 1986 **U**							125	150	200	200	200	300
0155/22	Santa's Elf, LE									100	100	125	225
0227/33	Schnuffy Bear Dressed, 1907 Rep, mhr, LE, 1987 **U**								1100	275	275		379
0118/00	Sleigh Set, mhr, LE 6000, 1989 **U**										275	275	350
0158/17	Snap-Apart Bear, mhr, LE 5000										135	275	300
2920/16	Snuffy Bear				29	29	29	31	38			50	56
2921/16	Snuffy Bear								42	56		60	67
0164/29	Somersault Bear, 1909 Rep, mhr, LE 5000, 1990 **W**											395	475
0156/38	St. Nicholas Bear, Vic. Santa Bxd, 1200 pc., 1987								150	200	200	200	300
0327/85	Standing Bear on 4 Legs								2963		4335	3895	4362
610158	(2) Steiff Bears plus Steiff Teddy Baren Book												750
0341/40	Super Molly Bear				90	90	90	95	125	170	170	170	190
0341/65	Super Molly Bear				185	185	185	195	250	350	350	350	392
0341/90	Super Molly Bear				300	300	300	320	400	600	600	600	672
0341/98	Super Molly Bear				450	450	450	475	575			785	879
0341/99	Super Molly Bear	600	680	700	700							920	1030
0438/70	Super Molly Panda						195	205	250			320	358
0438/98	Super Molly Panda						425	450	450			695	778
0324/60	Super Molly Teddy, Lying								395	525		525	588
0323/50	Super Molly Teddy, Standing								395	525		539	604
651854	T.R. The Toy Store, LE 1500, 1994 **U**												300
11979	Teddile, The Toy Store, LE 1000, 1992 **U**												275
5700/20	Teddy	39	43	43								85	95
5700/30	Teddy	57	62	62								120	134
6560/17	Teddy (Hand Puppet)											110	140
0177/00	Teddy Baby & Wolf Set, Zum 85 Jahrigen Jubilaum der Firma Paul Wolff, Grengen, LE 1000, 1988 **G**												650
420016	Teddy Baby Blue, Steiff Club, LE 7959, 1992 **G**												650
0177/19	Teddy Baby Food Vendor, mhr, LE 5000, 1990 **U**											140	175
0175/19	Teddy Baby Ringmaster, mhr, LE 5,000, 1989 **U**										140	140	200

Passport Teddy, 0245/40, yellow tag, 1985, $304.
Sheila Perry Collection.

Rub-A-Dub-Dub Set, 3 Bears in a Tub, 0131/00,
LE 2000, 1987, $350.
Sheila Perry Collection.

NEXT PAGE:
Top Photo:
(Left) Bride,
0155/36, LE 2000,
1984 on, $300.
(Right) Groom,
0155/37, LE 2000,
1984 on, $300.

Bottom Photo:
(Left) Ring Bearer,
0155/23, LE 2000,
1985-1988, $175.
(Right) Flower
Bearer, 0155/22,
LE 2000, 1985-
1988, $175.

Steiff #	Description	1980-1981	1981-1982	1982-1983	1983-1984	1984-1985	1985-1986	1986	1987	1988	1989	1990	Current
0179/19	Teddy Baby Rose, Hobby Center Toys, LE 1000, 1990 **U**												375
650529	Teddy Baby Ticket Seller, LE 5000, 1991 **U**												195
0176/29	Teddy Baby, 1930 Rep, blond, mhr, LE, 1985 **U**						95	100				245	200
0176/35	Teddy Baby, 1930 Rep, blond, mhr, LE, 1985 **U**						125	135	135			265	250
0176/42	Teddy Baby, 1930 Rep, blond, mhr, LE, 1985 **U**						175	185				400	350
0175/29	Teddy Baby, 1930 Rep, Brown, mhr, LE, 1984 **U**					85	95	100	125	175	175	175	275
0175/35	Teddy Baby, 1930 Rep, Brown, mhr, LE, 1984 **U**					110	125	135	165	225	225	225	350
0175/42	Teddy Baby, 1930 Rep, brown, mhr, LE, 1984 **U**					165	175	185	235	300	300	300	400
0246/80	Teddy Baby, Charcoal, WDW, LE 1, 1990 **U**											10350	N/P
8492/26	Teddy Bag					19	19	20	24	35		37	41
650925	Teddy Bar Eddi 27, Spiel & Spass, Baumwollsack, Germany, LE 2,000 **G**												N/P
0162/33	Teddy Bear 1906, FAO 125th Year Anniversary, LE 1,000, 1987 **U**												450
0270/28	Teddy Bear Bride, 1986 **W**							100	125	175		180	202
0271/28	Teddy Bear Groom, 1986 **W**							100	125			180	202
0148/03	Teddy Bear Pin				9							15	35
8500/03	Teddy Bear Pin					9	9	10	12	12		14	16
0276/28	Teddy Bear with Dirndl, 1986 **W**												225
0188/25	Teddy Bear, 1955 Rep, mit Halsmechanik, LE 4000, 1990 **W**												300
651526	Teddy Bear, 30cm, Blond, DL, LE 1500, 1993 **U**												400
651540	Teddy Bear, 80cm, Blond, DL, LE 5, 1993 **U**												N/P
651533	Teddy Bear. 60cm, Blond, DL, LE 25, 1993 **U**												N/P
420023	Teddy Clown 1928 Club Edition **W**												400
0163/19	Teddy Clown Junior, White Tag, LE **U**								50			195	225
0163/19	Teddy Clown Junior, Yellow Tag, LE 5000, 1987 **U**								50			125	175
0170/32	Teddy Clown, 1926 Rep, LE 10,000, 1986 **W**							150	150			395	400
6361/12	Teddy Coin Purse	10	11	12								22	25
651205	Teddy Donald, 30cm, WDW, LE 1500, 1993 **U**												550
651212	Teddy Donald, 60cm WDW, LE 25, 1993 **U**												3000
00206	Teddy Donald, 99cm, WDW, LE 2, 1993 **U**												N/P
0280/28	Teddy Dressed as a Sailor Boy, mhr, 1986 **W**							100	125	175	175	175	196
0281/28	Teddy Dressed as a Sailor Girl, mhr, 1986 **W**							100	125	175	175	175	196
0283/28	Teddy Dressed w/Black Forest Outfit, mhr, 1987 **W**								150	150		165	185
0284/28	Teddy Dressed w/Farmer Outfit, mhr, 1987 **W**								150	150		165	185
0276/28	Teddy Dressed with Lederhosen, mhr, 1986 **W**							100	125	175	175	175	196
8490/12	Teddy Minibag					12	12	12	15	22	22	23	25
0233/20	Teddy Petsy, Blonde					39	39	41	41			65	73
0233/28	Teddy Petsy, Blonde					50	50	53	65	95	95	63	71
0233/35	Teddy Petsy, Blonde					70	70	75	90	130	130	85	95
0233/45	Teddy Petsy, Blonde					100	100	105	140	190	190	120	134
0233/80	Teddy Petsy, Blonde						400	425	4100	4100		600	672
0235/20	Teddy Petsy, Cream					39	39	41	41			65	73
0235/28	Teddy Petsy, Cream					50	50	53	65	95	95	63	71
0235/35	Teddy Petsy, Cream					70	70	75	90	130	130	85	95
0235/45	Teddy Petsy, Cream					100	100	105	140	190	190	120	134
0230/20	Teddy Petsy, Rust					39	39					69	77
0230/28	Teddy Petsy, Rust					50	50	53	64	95	95	63	71
0230/35	Teddy Petsy, Rust					70	70	75	90	130	130	85	9
0230/45	Teddy Petsy, Rust					100	100	105	140	190	190	120	134
8494/03	Teddy Pin with Ribbon, mhr							20	19	19		22	25
8495/03	Teddy Pin, Beige, mhr					17	18	19	19			24	27

Steiff #	Description	1980-1981	1981-1982	1982-1983	1983-1984	1984-1985	1985-1986	1986	1987	1988	1989	1990	Current
8496/03	Teddy Pin, Caramel, mhr					17	18	19	19			24	27
8498/03	Teddy Pin, Chocolate, mhr					17	18	19	19	19		24	27
8497/03	Teddy Pin, White, mhr					17	18	19	19	19		24	27
0171/41	Teddy Rose w/Ctr. Seam, 1925, LE 10,000, 1987 **W**								1100	300	230	345	500
0171/25	Teddy Rose, LE											195	275
0167/23	Teddy Schwarz, 40th Birthday UFDC, LE 360, 1989 **U**												N/P
6360/12	Teddy Shoulder Bag	10	11	12	12							22	25
6365/26	Teddy Shoulder Bag, Lg.	17	19	19	19							34	38
0275/28	Teddy/Dr								100	125	175	175	196
11382	Teddys Teddy Baby, 19cm, Teddys, LE 1000, 1991 **U**												295
8472/17	Teeny Bag Panda								60	55		60	67
8470/17	Teeny Teddy Bag								60	77		80	90
0290/32	Toddel	43	50	51								100	112
6242/20	Toldi Bear			25	28							48	54
6242/30	Toldi Bear			49	53	53						90	101
6270/27	Toldi Bear									80		80	90
7580/27	Toldi Bear SOS										82	82	92
0211/36	Valentine Bear, mhr, **W**						60	64				175	236
0211/26	Valentine Bear, mhr, 1984						45	48				135	182
27086	Varsity Bear 35, Polo, Ralph Lauren, NY, 1994, LE 3,500 **U**												350
0155/35	Victorian Boy Bear 1986, LE 1200 **U**							125	125			225	250
0155/34	Victorian Girl Bear 1986, LE 1200 **U**							125				225	250
0166/29	W. Shakespeare Bear, 1909 Rep, LE 2,000, 1987 **E**												N/P
650581	Wellington Bear, Polo, Ralph Lauren, NY, 1994, LE 1500 **U**												450
0203/00	White Orig. Bears w/Paws, 5 pc.											625	844
0163/34	White Teddy Bear 1909, FAO Schwarz, LE 2000, 1988 **U**												350
0203/10	White Teddy Bear, Jointed, mhr, LE					35	36					88	125
0203/14	White Teddy Bear, Jointed, mhr, LE				25	30	30	30	30			75	135
0132/24	Wigwag Seesaw P-Toy w/Two Bears, mhr, LE 4000, 1988 **W**									260	260	260	260
651243	Winnie the Pooh, 30cm, WDW, LE 2500, 1994 **U**												700
651270	Winnie the Pooh, 80cm, WDW, LE, 1994 **U**												N/P
651250	Winnie the Pooh, 60cm, WDW, LE 25, 1994 **U**												N/P
0302/30	Zotty	60	67	70	70	70	70					110	123
0302/40	Zotty	85	95	98	98	98	98					160	179
0302/50	Zotty	125	140	145	145	145	145	155				230	258
0305/22	Zotty	34	40	41								200	224
0305/30	Zotty Bear							63	67	81	135	135	85	95
0305/40	Zotty Bear							95	100	125	200	200	125	140
0305/50	Zotty Bear							130	140	170	250	250	150	168
0305/32	Zotty, mhr	46	50	55								270	302
0305/45	Zotty, mhr	98	115	120								410	459

Key: W = World Wide • U = USA • E = England • G = Germany • WDW = Walt Disney World • DL = Disneyland • N/P = No prices available

Teddy Baby Blue, First Europe Steiff Club piece, 420016, LE, 1992. *Sheila Perry Collection.*

STEIFF COLLECTOR'S CLUB

Steiff #	Description	1980-1981	1981-1982	1982-1983	1983-1984	1984-1985	1985-1986	1986	1987	1988	1989	1990	Current
420016	Teddy Baby Blue, 1st Steiff Club, European, 1992												650
420023	Teddy Clown, 28cm, European & US Club, 1993												400
420047	Teddy Blue, 1908 Rep, 1994												N/P
420054	Baby Bear, Blond, 1946 Rep, Steiff Club, 1995												250
420801	Sam, 28cm, 1st US Steiff Club, 1993												750

Sam, First U.S. Steiff Club piece,
420801, LE 4643, 1993, $750.
Sheila Perry Collection.

Teddy Blue, 420047, 1908
Replica, 1994. *Sheila Perry
Collection.*

Key: W = World Wide
U = USA
E = England
G = Germany
WDW = Walt Disney World
DL = Disneyland
N/P = No prices available

Steiff #	Description	1980-1981	1981-1982	1982-1983	1983-1984	1984-1985	1985-1986	1986	1987	1988	1989	1990	Current
00206	Teddy Donald, 99cm, WDW, LE 2, 1993 U												N/P
011863	Minnie Bear, Black Margaret Strong Bear with white bib, WDW, LE 1500, 1992 U												650
011870	Minnie Bear, Black Margaret Strong Bear with White bib, 60cm, WDW, LE 20, 1992 U												2200
011863	Minnie Bear, Black Margaret Strong Bear with White bib, 80cm, WDW, LE 1, 1992 U												N/P
011863	Minnie Bear, Black Margaret Strong Bear with White Bib, 99cm, WDW, LE 1, 1992 U												N/P
011986	Antique Teddy, Grey, 30cm, DL, LE 1500, 1992 U												300
011993	Antique Teddy, Grey, 60cm, DL, LE 20, 1992 U												1500
012006	Antique Teddy, Grey, 80cm, DL, LE 1, 1992 U												N/P
012013	Antique Teddy, Grey, 99cm DL, LE 1, 1992 U												N/P
0243/32	Gold Bear w/Red Ribbon, mhr, WDW, LE, 1000, only 500 produced, 1988 U									95			750
0244/35	Petsy Bear, White, WDW, LE 1000, 1989 U										115		500
0245/32	Margaret Strong Bear, Grey mhr, WDW, LE 1000, 1990 U											125	400
0245/60	Margaret Strong Bear, WDW, LE 10, 1989 U												N/P
0245/80	Margaret Strong Bear, WDW, LE 1, 1989 U												N/P
0245/80	Petsy, 80cm, WDW, LE 1, 1990 U												N/P
0245/99	Petsy, 99cm, WDW, LE 1, 1990 U												N/P
0246/32	Mickey Bear, Black Margaret Strong Bear with Mickey Mouse Mask, 32cm, WDW, LE 1500, 1991 U												650
0246/60	Mickey Bear, Black Margaret Strong Bear with Mickey Mouse Mask, WDW, LE 1, 1991 U												3000
0246/80	Mickey Bear, Black Margaret Strong Bear with Mickey Mouse Mask, WDW, LE 1, 1991 U												N/P
0246/80	Teddy Baby, Charcoal, WDW, LE 1, 1990 U										10350		N/P
0246/99	Mickey Bear, Black Margaret Strong Bear with Mickey Mouse Mask, WDW, LE 1, 1991 U												N/P
651205	Teddy Donald, 30cm, WDW, LE 1500, 1993 U												550
651212	Teddy Donald, 60cm WDW, LE 25, 1993 U												3000
651243	Winnie the Pooh, 30cm, WDW, LE 2500, 1994 U												700
651250	Winnie the Pooh, 60cm, WDW, LE 25, 1994 U												N/P
651270	Winnie the Pooh, 80cm, WDW, LE, 1994 U												N/P
651526	Teddy Bear, 30cm, Blond, DL, LE 1500, 1993 U												400
651533	Teddy Bear, 60cm, Blond, DL, LE 25, 1993 U												N/P
651540	Teddy Bear, 80cm, Blond, DL, LE 5, 1993 U												N/P

Next Page:
Winnie the Pooh, 651243, LE 2500,
Walt Disney World, 1994, $700.
Sheila Perry Collection.

Key: W = World Wide • U = USA • E = England • G = Germany • WDW = Walt Disney World • DL = Disneyland • N/P = No prices available

1st Disney World Teddy
Bear Convention, 0243/32,
LE 500 pieces made (the tag
erronously states 1000),
1988, $750.
Note special
Disney World logo.

Minnie Bear, 011863,
LE 20, Walt Disney
World, 1992. *Sheila
Perry Collection.*

Teddy Baby, 024680, Charcoal, LE 1, Walt Disney World,
1990. *Sheila Perry Collection.*

Teddy Donald, 651205, LE 1500, Walt Disney World, 1993,
$550. *Sheila Perry Collection.*

3rd Disney World Teddy Bear Convention, 011429,
Charcoal, LE 1000, 1990. *Sheila Perry Collection.*

2nd Disney World Teddy Bear Convention, 0244/35, White,
LE 1000, 1989, $500. *Sheila Perry Collection.*

Mickey Bear (0246/32) $650 and Minnie Bear (011863), $650, Disney World Teddy Bear Convention, LE, 1992-1993. *Sheila Perry Collection.*

2nd Disneyland 1993 Gold Musical plays
"When You Wish Upon A Star", 651526,
LE 1500, 1993.
Sheila Perry Collection.

1st Disneyland 1992 Light Grey, 011986,
LE 2000, 1992, $300.
Sheila Perry Collection.

Teddy's Teddy Baby, 011382, 19cm, made especially for Teddys, 1991, $295. *Sheila Perry Collection.*

SPECIAL EDITIONS

Steiff #	Description	1980-1981	1981-1982	1982-1983	1983-1984	1984-1985	1985-1986	1986	1987	1988	1989	1990	Current
4003	Goldilocks 16" & 3 Steiff Bears, Reeves International, (0173/25, Boy; 0173/30, Mother; 0173/32, Father), 1984, Offered at $200 **U**												750
4004	Goldilocks 8" & 3 Steiff Bears, Reeves International, 0173/25, Boy; 0173/18, Mother; 0173/22 Father), 1985, Offered at $200 **U**												450
4005	Alice & Her Friends, (13cm Steiff Cat; 13cm Steiff Mouse; 20cm Steiff Rabbit w/big pocket watch), LE 3000, 1986, Offered at $250 **U**												400
011382	Teddys Teddy Baby, 19cm, Teddys LE 1000, 1991 **U**												295
011979	Teddile, The Toy Store, LE 1000, 1992 **U**												275
0128/33	Bear w/Snow White & Rose Red Set, Suzanne Gibson Doll Reeves International, 1987, LE 2000 **U**												400
0140/38	Klein Archie, Enchanted Dollhouse, LE 2500 **U**												175
0151/27	Harrods Musical Bear 1904/05, LE 2000, 1990 **E**												395
0152/25	Mr. Vanilla, Hobby Center Toys, LE 1000, 1989 **U**												475
0159/26	Antique Teddy Schwarz, J.P. Bear, Mary D's Dolls & Bears & Such, LE 1000, 1990 **U**												275
0162/33	Teddy Bear 1906, FAO 125th Year Anniversary, LE 1,000, 1987 **U**												450
0163/26	Hamleys Bear, LE 2000, 1988 **E**												350
0163/34	White Teddy Bear 1909, FAO Schwarz, LE 2000, 1988 **U**												350
0166/32	Preppy Bear 35 (blue shirt, pants & sweater), Polo, Ralph Lauren, NY, 1991/92 **U**												350

FAO Musical Teddy Bear,
652080, LE 2000, 1993.
Sheila Perry Collection.

Key: W = World Wide
U = USA
E = England
G = Germany
WDW = Walt Disney World
DL = Disneyland
N/P = No prices available

39

SPECIAL EDITIONS

Steiff #	Description	1980-1981	1981-1982	1982-1983	1983-1984	1984-1985	1985-1986	1986	1987	1988	1989	1990	Current
0167/23	Teddy Schwarz, 40th Birthday UFDC, LE 360, 1989 **U**												N/P
0168/28	Hamleys Bear, LE 2000, 1989 **E**												250
0172/18	Dicky Bear Rose, The Toy Store, LE 1000, 1991, (set) **U**												300
0172/19	Dicky Bear Mauve, The Toy Store, LE 1000, 1991, (set) **U**												300
0172/32	Dicky "Clowns Around", Ronald McDonald House **U**												650
0173/14	Goldilock Bear Boy (part of set #4004), LE, 1985 **U**												150
0173/18	Goldilock Bear Mother (part of set #4004), LE, 1985 **U**												200
0173/22	Goldilock Bear Boy (part of set #4004), LE, 1985 **U**												175
0173/25	Goldilock Bear Father (part of set #4004), LE, 1985 **U**												200
0173/30	Goldilock Bear Mother (part of set #4003), LE, 1984 **U**												250
0177/00	Teddy Baby and Wolf Set, Zum 85 Jahrigen Jubilaum der Firma Paul Wolff, Grengen, LE 1000, 1988 **G**												650
0179/19	Teddy Baby Rose, Hobby Center Toys, LE 1000, 1990 **U**												375
0181/36	Hamleys Bear Oliver, LE 2000, 1990 **E**												N/P
0184/35	Alfonzo, Teddy Bears of Whitney, LE 5000, 1990 **E**												500
	Nicholaus Bar, Hobby Center Toys, LE 300, 1985 **U**												450
	Frau Nikolaus, Hobby Center Toys, LE 150, 1986 **U**												400
0201/14	Hans Helfer, Hobby Center Toys, LE 200, 1987 **U**												250
0218/14	Gieng-Ling Panda, Hobby Center Toys, LE 1000, 1988 **U**												400
0260/25	Jackie Bear Rose, Doll House Southern Bear, LE 1000, 1990 **U**												273
027062	Preppy Bear 35, Polo, Ralph Lauren, NY, 1994 **U**												350
027079	Chairman II Bear 43, Polo, Ralph Lauren, NY, 1994, LE 1,500 **U**												800

J.P. Bear, Mary D's Dolls & Bears & Such, 650376, LE 1000, 1990. *Sheila Perry Collection.*

Key: W = World Wide
U = USA
E = England
G = Germany
WDW = Walt Disney World
DL = Disneyland
N/P = No prices available

SPECIAL EDITIONS

Steiff #	Description	1980-1981	1981-1982	1982-1983	1983-1984	1984-1985	1985-1986	1986	1987	1988	1989	1990	Current
027086	Varsity Bear 35, Polo, Ralph Lauren, NY, 1994, LE 3500 **U**												350
027093	Producer Bear 43, Polo, Ralph Lauren, NY, 1994, LE 1500 **U**												800
0277/28	Hans, Marshall Fields, 1985 **U**												300
0278/28	Helga, Marshall Fields, 1985 **U**												300
0285/29	Golden Gate Bear, FAO Schwarz/ San Francisco, LE 2000, 1989 **U**												600
0291/26	Harrods Musical Bear 1909, LE 2000, 1989 **E**												375
0294/42	Harrods Musical Bear 1920, Elise von Beethoven, LE 2000, 1991 **E**												N/P
0296/38	Hamleys Tobias mit musikwerk, LE 2000, 1992 **E**												350
1232/25	Mohair Soft Schwarzbear (Black Bear Cup), FAO Schwarz, (North American Wildlife Series), LE 2000, 1990 **U**												250
406225	American Flag Bear, 35cm, Polo, Ralph Lauren, NY, LE 3500, 1992 **U**												425
600393	Martini Bear, Polo, Ralph Lauren, NY, LE 1500, 1994 **U**												800

Luxury Edition Steiff Book with two bears, LE 250 U.S., LE 1000 European. *Sheila Perry Collection.*

The Preppy Bear, 27062, Polo, Ralph Lauren Collection, yellow, 1991. *Maryann DiIorio.*

Martini Bear, 600393, Polo, Ralph Lauren Collection, yellow, 1994, $800. *Sheila Perry Collection.*

American Flag Bear, 406225, Polo, Ralph Lauren Collection, LE 3500, 1992, $425. *Maryann DiIoria.*

SPECIAL EDITIONS

Harrods Musical Bear, 1920, for Elise von Beethoven, 0294/42, LE 2000, England, 1991. *Sheila Perry Collection.*

Hamleys Tobias, 011948, LE 2000, England, 1992. *Sheila Perry Collection.*

Alfonzo, 0184/35, Teddy Bears of Whitney, LE 5,000, England, 1990. Sheila Perry Collection.

SPECIAL EDITIONS

Steiff #	Description	1980-1981	1981-1982	1982-1983	1983-1984	1984-1985	1985-1986	1986	1987	1988	1989	1990	Current
650581	Wellington Bear, Polo, Ralph Lauren, NY, LE 1500, 1994 **U**												450
650581	Russia Bear, Polo, Ralph Lauren, NY, LE 1500, 1994 **U**												350
650680	Harrods Musical Bear 1906, LE 2,000, 1993 **E**												400
650918	Original Teddy Bar 36, Spielzeug Ring, Baumwoll-sack, Germany, LE 3000 **W**												N/P
650925	Teddy bar Eddi 27, Spiel & Spass, Baumwollsack, Germany, LE 2,000 **G**												N/P
651847	Petsile, The Toy Store, LE 1000, 1993 **U**												195
651854	T.R., The Toy Store, LE 1,500, 1994 **U**												300
651861	Golli G. & Teddi B., The Toy Store, LE 1500, 1995 **U**												400
651878	Molly Golli & Peg, The Toy Store, LE 2500, 1996 **U**												225
652080	Musikteddy 33, FAO Schwarz, LE 2000, 1993 **U**												350
999765	Amelia, (with fliers coat/hat/goggles), I. Magnin, LE 650, 1993 **U**												600

Next Page: Hobby Center and The Toy Store Exclusives from Top left to right: Nicholaus, $450, and Frau Nicholaus, $400, LE 150, 1987; Hans Helfer, 0201/14, LE 200, 1987, $250; Gieng-Ling Panda, 0218/14, LE 1000, 1988, $400. Center Left to right: Mr. Vanilla, 0152/25, LE 1000, 1989, $475; Teddy Baby Rose, 0179/19, LE 1000, 1990, $375; Dicky Rose, 0172/18 and Dicky Mauve, 0172/19, LE 1000, 1991, $300 a set; Teddile 011979, LE 1000, 1992, $275. Bottom left to right: Petsile, 651847, LE 1000, 1993, $195; T.R., 651854, LE 1500, 1994, $300; Golli G & Teddy B, 651861, LE 1500, 1995, $400; Molly Golli & Peg, 651878, LE 2500, 1996, $225.

Key: W = World Wide • U = USA • E = England • G = Germany • WDW = Walt Disney World • DL = Disneyland • N/P = No prices available

SPECIAL EDITIONS

Santa, 0155/38, yellow tag, 1986, $300. *Sheila Perry Collection.*

TEDDY BEARS – NUMERICAL

Steiff #	Description	1980-1981	1981-1982	1982-1983	1983-1984	1984-1985	1985-1986	1986	1987	1988	1989	1990	Current
4003	Goldilocks 16" & 3 Steiff Bears, Reeves International, (0173/25, Boy; 0173/30, Mother; 0173/32, Father), 1984, Offered at $200 **U**												750
4004	Goldilocks 8" & 3 Steiff Bears, Reeves International, 0173/25. Boy; 0173/18, Mother; 0173/22 Father), 1985, Offered at $200 **U**												450
4005	Alice & Her Friends, (13cm Steiff Cat; 13cm Steiff Mouse; 20cm Steiff Rabbit w/big pocket watch), LE 3000, 1986, Offered at $250 **U**												400
00206	Teddy Donald, 99cm, WDW, LE 2, 1993 **U**												N/P
120/19	Bear Band Leader w/Baton, LE									125	125	135	195
51847	Petsil, The Toy Store, LE, 1500, 1993 **U**												175
0082/20	Roly Poly Bear, 1894, 2 yr LE					69	70	70	70	80	80	95	150
0085/12	Bear on Wheels, LE 12,000						95	100	100	120	120	165	175
0090/11	Polar Bear Jntd Legs/Rtng Head, LE 3000							95	95			155	200
0100/90	Circus Wagon w/Two Bears, LE										450		475
011382	Teddys Teddy Baby, 19cm, Teddys LE 1000, 1991 **U**												295
0115/18	Roly Poly Bear w/Rattle 1908, mhr, LE									125	125	125	145
0116/25	Record Teddy, 1913, LE 4000, 1990 **W**											300	350
0118/00	Sleigh Set, mhr, LE 6000, 1989 **U**										275	275	350
011863	Minnie Bear, WDW, LE 1500, 1992 **U**												650
011863	Minnie Bear, 80cm, WDW, LE 1, 1992 **U**												N/P
011863	Minnie Bear, 99cm, WDW, LE 1, 1992 **U**												N/P
011870	Minnie Bear, 60cm, WDW, LE 20, 1992 **U**												2200

Teddy "Jackie," 1953 Replica, 0190/25, LE 10,000 pieces, 1986-1987, $275.

Key: **W** = World Wide
U = USA
E = England
G = Germany
WDW = Walt Disney World
DL = Disneyland
N/P = No prices available

47

Steiff #	Description	1980-1981	1981-1982	1982-1983	1983-1984	1984-1985	1985-1986	1986	1987	1988	1989	1990	Current
011979	Teddile, The Toy Store, LE 1000, 1992 **U**												275
011986	Antique Teddy, Grey, 30cm, DL, LE 1500, 1992 **U**												300
011993	Antique Teddy, Grey, 60cm, DL, LE 20, 1992 **U**												1500
012006	Antique Teddy, Grey, 80cm, DL, LE 1, 1992 **U**												N/P
012013	Antique Teddy, Grey, 99cm DL, LE 1, 1992 **U**												N/P
0120/19	Bear Band Leader, LE 5000, 1988 **U**												185
0120/19	Bear Band Leader w/ Baton, LE									125	125	135	195
0128/33	Bear w/Snow White & Rose Red Set, Suzanne Gibson Doll Reeves International, 1987, LE 2000 **U**												400
0130/28	Bear on 4 Legs, Univ. Head Mov., mhr, LE 4000									400	400		550
0131/00	Rub-A-Dub-Dub Set, 3 Bears in a Tub, LE 2000, 1988 **U**								275	275		310	350
0131/23	Rub-A-Dub-Dub Set, yellow, Baker, LE 2000 **U**												140
0131/24	Rub-A-Dub-Dub Set, brass, Candlemaker, LE 2000, 1988 **U**												140
0131/25	Rub-A-Dub-Dub Set, brown butcher, LE 2000, 1988 **U**												140
0132/24	Wigwag Seesaw P-Toy w/Two Bears, mhr, LE 4000, 1988 **W**									260	260	260	260
0135/20	Baby Bear Pull Toy w/wagon, 1908 Rep, LE 4000 **W**										275	275	300
0140/38	Klein Archie, Enchanted Dollhouse, LE 2500 **U**												175
0148/03	Teddy Bear Pin				9						15		35
0150/32	Richard Steiff 1902-1903 Bear, LE 20,000 **W**				90	100					285		400
0151/25	Mr. Cinnamon Bear, (1904), LE, 1984 **U**					70	75	79			165		275
0151/26	Mr. Cinnamon Bear, 1984 **U**												275

Brummbar, 0228/48, yellow tag, 1988, $338.
Sheila Perry Collection.

Key: W = World Wide
U = USA
E = England
G = Germany
WDW = Walt Disney World
DL = Disneyland
N/P = No prices available

TEDDY BEARS – NUMERICAL

Steiff #	Description	1980-1981	1981-1982	1982-1983	1983-1984	1984-1985	1985-1986	1986	1987	1988	1989	1990	Current
0151/27	Harrods Musical Bear 1904/05, LE 2000, 1990 E												395
0151/32	Mr. Cinnamon Bear, (1904), LE, 1984 U					85	90	95				265	350
0151/40	Mr. Cinnamon Bear, (1904), LE, 1984 U					125	135	145				435	450
0151/55	Mr. Cinnamon Bear, (1904), LE, 1985 U												500
0152/25	Mr. Vanilla, Hobby Center Toys, LE 1000, 1989 U												475
0153/43	Papa Bar, 100th Annv, LE 5,000,												
	Original Teddy U	150										800	1000
0155/15	Christening Bear, 1986, LE U							60	75	75		99	150
0155/18	Roly Poly Bear with rattle, 1908 Rep, 1990 U												150
0155/22	Santa's Elf, LE									100	100	125	225
0155/22	Flower Bear-er, LE 2000 pc, 1985 U						75	80	100	100		125	175
0155/23	Ring Bear-er, LE 2000 pc. 1985 U						75	80	100	100		125	175
0155/26	Margaret Strong Bear, mhr, LE, 1984 U			48	48	50	53	56	69	100	100	100	120
0155/32	Margaret Strong Bear, mhr, LE, 1984 U			62	62	65	69	73	89	135	135	135	160
0155/34	Victorian Girl Bear 1986, LE 1200 U							125				225	250
0155/35	Victorian Boy Bear 1986, LE 1200 U							125	125			225	250
0155/36	Bride, LE 2000, 1984 U					100	110	125	150	200	200	215	300
0155/37	Groom, LE 2000, 1984 U					100	110	125	150	200	200	215	300
0155/38	Mama & Baby, mhr, LE 8,000, 7500 U		150									495	600
0155/38	Santa Bear, 1000 pc., 1986 U							125	150	200	200	200	300
0155/42	Margaret Strong Bear, mhr, LE, 1983 U				90	95	100	105	125	200	200	200	240
0155/51	Margaret Strong Gold Bear, mhr, LE, 1983 U					185	195	205	250	350	350	350	360
0155/60	Margaret Strong Gold Bear, mhr, LE, 1984 U					250	285	300	375	495	495	495	425
0156/00	Margaret Strong Cinnamon Bear Set, mhr,												
	LE 2,000, 1984 U					300	300					590	900
0156/26	Cinnamon Bear, mhr, LE							53				100	250

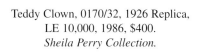

Teddy Clown, 0170/32, 1926 Replica,
LE 10,000, 1986, $400.
Sheila Perry Collection.

Teddy Bears – Numerical

Steiff #	Description	1980-1981	1981-1982	1982-1983	1983-1984	1984-1985	1985-1986	1986	1987	1988	1989	1990	Current
0156/32	Cinnamon Bear, mhr							69				135	350
0156/34	Captain Strong Bear, 1987, LE **U**									200	200	215	275
0156/36	M. Strong Victorian Lady, L.E. 1987 **U**								150	150	150	195	250
0156/37	M. Strong Victorian Gentleman, LE, 1987 **U**								150	150	150	195	250
0156/38	St. Nicholas Bear, Vic. Santa Bxd, 1200 pc., 1987								150	200	200	200	300
0156/42	Cinnamon Bear, mhr, LE							100				195	450
0157/26	Margaret Strong Cream Bear, mhr, LE, 1984 **U**					50	53	56				145	250
0157/32	Margaret Strong Cream Bear, mhr, LE, 1984 **U**					65	69	73				185	350
0157/42	Margaret Strong Cream Bear, Mhr, LE 1984 **U**					95	100	105				265	450
0157/51	Margaret Strong Cream Bear, mhr, LE, 1985 **U**						195	205				565	700
0157/60	Margaret Strong Cream Bear, mhr, LE, 1985 **U**						285	300				625	1200
0158/17	Snap-Apart Bear, mhr, LE 5000										135	275	300
0158/25	Margaret Strong White Bear, Leather Paws, mhr, LE 3000 **U**							60	60	60		165	400
0158/31	Margaret Strong White Bear, Leather Paws, mhr, LE 2500 **U**							79	79	79		255	600
0158/41	Margaret Strong White Bear, Leather Paws, mhr, LE 2000 **U**							110	110	110		325	1000
0158/50	Margaret Strong White Bear, Leather Paws, mhr, LE 750 **U**							225				1200	1600
0159/26	Antique Teddy Schwarz, J.P. Bear, Mary D's Dolls & Bears & Such, LE 1000, 1990 **U**												275
0160/00	M. Strong Choc. Brown Set, 4pc. L.E. 2,000 **U**				275							480	850
0162/00	Giengen Teddy Set, "The Birthplace of the Teddy," LE, 1600 1984 **W**					150	159	159	159			260	375
0162/33	Teddy Bear 1906, FAO 125th Year Anniversary, LE 1,000, 1987 **U**												450

Manschli, 0130/19, yellow tag, 1983/1984. Even though this is a yellow tag bear, it is hard to find because it was produced for such a short time. *Sheila Perry Collection*.

Key: W = World Wide
U = USA
E = England
G = Germany
WDW = Walt Disney World
DL = Disneyland
N/P = No prices available

TEDDY BEARS – NUMERICAL

Steiff #	Description	1980-1981	1981-1982	1982-1983	1983-1984	1984-1985	1985-1986	1986	1987	1988	1989	1990	Current
0163/19	Teddy Clown Junior, White Tag, LE U								50			195	225
0163/19	Teddy Clown Junior, Yellow Tag, LE 5000 1987 U								50			125	175
0163/20	Clown Teddy, mhr, LE 5000										100	100	175
0163/26	Hamleys Bear, LE 2000, 1988 E												350
0163/34	White Teddy Bear 1909, FAO Schwarz, LE 2000, 1988 U												350
0164/29	Somersault Bear, 1909 Rep, mhr, LE 5000, 1990 W											395	475
0164/30	Circus Dolly Bear (Rare Pale Yellow) 1987 approx. 800 Pieces								135			245	375
0164/31	Circus Dolly Bear/ Yellow, mhr, LE 2000 white tag, 1987 U								135	175	175	185	250
0164/32	Circus Dolly Bear/Green, mhr, LE 2000 white tag, 1987 U								135	175	175	185	250
0164/34	Circus Dolly Bear/Violet, mhr, LE 2000 white tag, 1987 U								135	175	175	185	250
0165/28	1909 Gold Teddy, mhr, 1983 W					55	59	62	62			75	270
0165/38	1909 Gold Teddy Bear, mhr, 1983 W				80	85	90	95				110	358
0165/51	1909 Gold Teddy, mhr, 1983 W					150	159	169				435	587
0165/60	1909 Gold Teddy, mhr, 1984 W						275	290	290			580	945
0166/25	Blond Teddy, 1909, mhr, 1988 W									100	100	100	134

Polar Bear, 0090/11, 1909 Replica, Museum Collection, LE 3900, 1987, $200. *Sheila Perry Collection.*

TEDDY BEARS – NUMERICAL

Steiff #	Description	1980-1981	1981-1982	1982-1983	1983-1984	1984-1985	1985-1986	1986	1987	1988	1989	1990	Current
0166/29	W. Shakespeare Bear, 1909 Rep, LE 2,000, 1987 **E**												N/P
0166/32	Preppy Bear 35, Polo, Ralph Lauren, NY, 1991/92 **U**												350
0166/35	Blond Teddy, 1909, mhr, 1988 **W**									145	145	145	196
0166/43	Blond Teddy, 1909, mhr, 1988 **W**									225	225	225	304
0167/22	Giengen Bear, Grey, 1906 Rep, mhr, 1986 **U**							55	69	100	100	100	150
0167/23	Teddy Schwarz, 40th Birthday UFDC, LE 360, 1989 **U**												N/P
0167/26	Giengen Teddy Bear Grey, 1906 Rep, 1985 **U**												185
0167/32	Giengen Bear, Grey, 1906 Rep, mhr, 1985 **U**						85	90	100	160	160	160	225
0167/42	Giengen Bear, Grey, 1906 Rep, mhr, 1985 **U**						120	125	150	225	225	225	350
0167/52	Giengen Bear, Grey, 1906 Rep, mhr, 1986 **U**							195	250	350	350	350	140
0168/22	Giengen Bear, Blond, 1906 Rep, mhr,1986 **U**							55	69	100	100	100	140
0168/28	Hamleys Bear, LE 2000, 1989 **E**												250
0168/32	Giengen Teddy Bear, Blond, 1988 **W**												225
0168/42	Giengen Bear, Blond, 1906 Rep, mhr, 1986 **U**							125	150	225		235	300
0169/65	Happy Anniversary, 1926 Rep, LE 5000, 1990 **U**											525	1100
0170/32	Teddy Clown, 1926 Rep, LE 10,000, 1986 **W**							150	150			395	400
0171/25	Teddy Rose, LE											195	275
0171/41	Teddy Rose w/Ctr. Seam, 1925, LE 10,000, 1987 **W**								1100	300	230	345	500
0172/17	Dicky Bear blond (for Circus wagon), LE 5000, 1990 **U**												130

Panda, 0178/35, $350, 0178/29, $250, yellow tags, 1984.
Nadine Gravatt Collection.

Key: W = World Wide
U = USA
E = England
G = Germany
WDW = Walt Disney World
DL = Disneyland
N/P = No prices available

TEDDY BEARS – NUMERICAL

Steiff #	Description	1980-1981	1981-1982	1982-1983	1983-1984	1984-1985	1985-1986	1986	1987	1988	1989	1990	Current
0172/18	Dicky Bear Rose, The Toy Store, LE 1000, 1991, (set) **U**												300
0172/19	Dicky Bear Mauve, The Toy Store, LE 1000, 1991, (set) **U**												300
0172/32	Dicky Bear, 1930 Rep, LE 20,000, 1985 **W**						100	105	105	125		225	275
0172/32	Dicky "Clowns Around", Ronald McDonald House **U**												650
0173/14	Goldilock Bear Boy (part of set #4004), LE, 1985 **U**												150
0173/18	Goldilock Bear Mother (part of set #4004), LE												200
0173/22	Goldilock Bear Boy (part of set #4004), LE, 1985 **U**												175
0173/25	Goldilock Bear Father, (part of set #4004), LE, 1985 **U**												200
0173/30	Goldilock Bear Mother, (part of set #4003), LE 1984 **U**												250
0173/32	Goldilocks Bear, Father (part of set #4003), LE, 1984 **U**												275
0173/40	Black Bear, 1907 Rep, LE 4000, 1988 **W**									300	300	600	800
0174/35	Muzzle Bear, White, 1908 Rep, LE 6000, 1990 **W**											295	270
0174/46	Muzzle Bear, White, 1908 Rep, mhr, LE 5000, 1989 **U**									375	375	375	450
0174/60	Muzzle Bear, White, 1908 Rep, mhr, LE 2650, 1989 **U**										500	500	700
0174/61	British Collectors Bear, LE 2000, 1989 **E**												800
0175/19	Teddy Baby Ringmaster, mhr, LE 5,000, 1989 **U**										140	140	200
0175/29	Teddy Baby, 1930 Rep, Brown, mhr, LE, 1984 **U**					85	95	100	125	175	175	175	275
0175/35	Teddy Baby, 1930 Rep, Brown, mhr., LE, 1984 **U**					110	125	135	165	225	225	225	350
0175/42	Teddy Baby, 1930 Rep, brown, mhr., LE, 1984 **U**					165	175	185	235	300	300	300	400
0176/29	Teddy Baby, 1930 Rep, blond, mhr., LE, 1985 **U**						95	100				245	200
0176/35	Teddy Baby, 1930 Rep, blond, mhr., LE, 1985 **U**						125	135	135			265	250
0176/42	Teddy Baby, 1930 Rep, blond, mhr., LE, 1985 **U**						175	185				400	350
0177/00	Teddy Baby & Wolf Set, Zum 85 Jahrigen Jubilaum der Firma Paul Wolff, Grengen, LE 1000, 1988 **G**												650

Record Teddy, 0116/25,
1913 Replica,
Museum Collection,
LE 4000, 1990, $350.
Sheila Perry Collection.

Teddy Bears – Numerical

Steiff #	Description	1980-1981	1981-1982	1982-1983	1983-1984	1984-1985	1985-1986	1986	1987	1988	1989	1990	Current
0177/19	Teddy Baby Food Vendor, mhr, LE 5000, 1990 **U**											140	175
0178/29	1938 Panda, mhr, LE					85	85					265	250
0178/35	1938 Panda, mhr, LE					110	110					320	350
0179/19	Teddy Baby Rose, Hobby Center Toys, LE 1000, 1990 **U**												375
0180/50	Petsy Bear, Ctr. Seam Bicolor, mhr, LE 5000, 1989/90 **U**										375	375	700
0181/35	Petsy Bear, Rep Ctr Seam Brass, mhr, LE 5000 **W**										225	225	395
0181/36	Hamleys Bear Oliver, LE 2000, 1990 **E**												N/P
0184/35	Alfonzo, Teddy Bears of Whitney, LE 5000, 1990 **E**												500
0188/25	Teddy Bear, 1955 Rep, mit Halsmechanik, LE 4000, 1990 **W**												300
0190/17	Jackie Bear, 1953 Rep, mhr, LE 12,000 **W**										135	135	175
0190/25	Jackie Bear, 1953 Rep, mhr, LE 10,000, 1987 **W**							110	135			295	275
0190/35	Jackie Bear, 1953 Rep, mhr, LE 4000, 1988 **U**									300	300	300	350
0201/10	Beige Teddy Bear, Jointed, mhr, LE					35	36					88	100
0201/11	Original Teddy, Beige, mhr	9	10	13	15	19	20	21	25	30	30	30	70
0201/14	Beige Teddy Bear, Jointed, mhr, LE				25	30	30					75	125
	Nicholaus Bar, Hobby Center Toys, LE 300, 1985 **U**												450
	Frau Nikolaus, Hobby Center Toys, LE 150, 1986 **U**												400
0201/14	Hans Helfer, Hobby Center Toys, LE 200, 1987 **U**												250
0201/18	Original Teddy, Beige, mhr				30	35	37	39	47	70	70	70	125
0201/26	Original Teddy, Beige, mhr	27	30	33	36	40	43	45	55	85	85	85	150
0201/36	Original Teddy, Beige, mhr	36	40	48	50	55	59	62	75	115	115	115	225
0201/41	Original Teddy Bear, Beige, mhr			70	75	75	79	85	100	160	160	160	275
0201/51	Original Teddy Bear, Beige, mhr			115	120	120	125	135	165	250	250	250	350
0201/75	Original Teddy Bear, Beige, mhr				450	500	529	560	675	975	975	975	1300
0201/99	Original Bear Beige, mhr			700	700	750	795	850	9100	1450		2300	3000
0202/10	Caramel Teddy Bear, Jointed, mhr, LE					35	36					88	100
0202/11	Original Teddy, Caramel, mhr	9	10	13	15	19	20	21	25	30	30	30	70

(Right) Teddy Clown Jr, 0163/20,
LE 3000, 1989, $175.
(Left) Teddy Clown Jr, 0163/19,
LE 2000, 1987, $225.
Sheila Perry Collection.

Key: W = World Wide
U = USA
E = England
G = Germany
WDW = Walt Disney World
DL = Disneyland
N/P = No prices available

TEDDY BEARS – NUMERICAL

Steiff #	Description	1980-1981	1981-1982	1982-1983	1983-1984	1984-1985	1985-1986	1986	1987	1988	1989	1990	Current
0202/12	Original Teddy, Caramel, Mini-Mohair										50	50	70
0202/14	Caramel Teddy Bear, Jointed, mhr, LE U				25	30	30					75	125
0202/15	Original Teddy, Caramel, Mini-Mohair										70	70	100
0202/18	Original Teddy, Caramel, mhr				30	35	37	39	47	70	70	70	125
0202/26	Original Teddy, Caramel, mhr	27	30	33	36	40	43	45	55	85	85	85	150
0202/36	Original Teddy, Caramel, mhr	36	40	48	50	55	59	62	75	115	115	115	225
0202/41	Original Teddy, Caramel, mhr	53	60	70	75	75	79	85	100	160	160	160	275
0202/51	Original Teddy, Caramel, mhr	84	100	115	120	120	125	135	165	250	250	250	350
0202/75	Original Teddy, Caramel, mhr				450	500	529	560	675	975		1195	1300
0202/99	Original Teddy, Caramel, mhr				700	750	795	850	9100	1450		2300	3105
0203/00	White Orig. Bears w/Paws, 5 pc.											625	844
0203/10	White Teddy Bear, Jointed, mhr, LE					35	36					88	125
0203/11	Original Teddy Bear, White, mhr			13	15	19	20	21	25			39	80
0203/14	White Teddy Bear, Jointed, mhr, LE				25	30	30	30	30			75	135
0203/18	Original Teddy White, mhr				30	35	37	39	47			87	152
0203/26	Original Teddy Bear, White, mhr			33	36	40	43	45	55			110	192
0203/36	Original Teddy Bear, White, mhr			48	50	55	59	62	75			175	306
0203/41	Original Teddy Bear, White, mhr			70	75	75	79	85	100			235	411
0203/51	Original Teddy Bear, White, mhr				120	120	125	135	165			310	543
0203/75	Original Teddy Bear, White, mhr				450	500						1250	1688
0203/99	Original Teddy Bear, White, mhr				700	750						2800	3780
0204/16	1982 The Teddy Tea Party, LE 10,000 U			175								300	675
0205/26	Original Teddy, Caramel	32	35	37	37	45	45	48	58			80	108
0205/35	Original Teddy, Caramel	45	50	52	54	62	62	66	80			110	149
0205/50	Original Teddy, Caramel	97	105	120	120	120						235	317
0206/10	Chocolate Teddy Bear, Jointed, mhr, LE					35	36					88	119

Petsy Bicolor, 0180/50, 1927
Replica, LE 5000, 1989-1990, $700.
Sheila Perry Collection.

TEDDY BEARS – NUMERICAL

Steiff #	Description	1980-1981	1981-1982	1982-1983	1983-1984	1984-1985	1985-1986	1986	1987	1988	1989	1990	Current
0206/11	Original Teddy, Choc. Brown, mhr					19	20	21	25	30	30	30	65
0206/14	Chocolate Teddy Bear, Jointed, mhr, LE					30	30	30				75	125
0206/18	Original Teddy, Chocolate Brown, mhr					35	37	39	47	70	70	70	123
0206/26	Original Teddy, Chocolate Brown, mhr					40	43	45	55	85	85	85	149
0206/36	Original Teddy, Chocolate Brown, mhr					55	59	62	75	115	115	115	201
0206/41	Original Teddy, Chocolate Brown, mhr					75	79	85	100	160	160	160	280
0206/51	Original Teddy, Chocolate Brown, mhr					120	125	135	165	250	250	250	438
0207/10	Grey Teddy Bear, mhr, LE						36	38	38			88	119
0207/12	Original Teddy, Grey, mhr											50	67
0207/14	Grey Teddy Bear, mhr, LE						30					75	101
0207/15	Original Teddy, Grey, mhr											70	94
0207/26	Original Teddy, Grey, mhr, LE							45	45	85	85	85	149
0207/36	Original							62	62	115	115	115	201
0207/41	Original Teddy, Grey, mhr, LE							85	85	160	160	160	280
0208/10	Black Teddy Bear, mhr, LE						36	38	38			88	119
0208/14	Black Teddy Bear, mhr, LE						30					75	125
0209/12	Original Teddy, Black, mhr											50	67
0209/15	Original Teddy, Black, mhr											70	125
0210/12	Original Teddy, Blond, Mini-Mohair										50	50	67
0210/15	Original Teddy, Blond, Mini-Mohair										70	70	125
0210/22	Nimrod Teddy Set, Teddy Roosevelt Comm. Set, mhr, LE 10,000 U				1100							275	550

Bear on 4 legs, univ. head movement, 0130/28, LE 4000, 1989-1990, $550.

Key: W = World Wide
U = USA
E = England
G = Germany
WDW = Walt Disney World
DL = Disneyland
N/P = No prices available

Teddy Bears – Numerical

Steiff #	Description	1980-1981	1981-1982	1982-1983	1983-1984	1984-1985	1985-1986	1986	1987	1988	1989	1990	Current
0211/10	Original Teddy, Rose, LE 8000											60	81
0211/12	Original Teddy, Rose, mhr											50	67
0211/15	Original Teddy, Rose, mhr											70	94
0211/26	Valentine Bear, mhr, 1984					45		48				135	182
0211/36	Valentine Bear, mhr, **W**					60		64				175	236
0212/10	Original Teddy, Cream, mhr, LE							38	38			82	111
0213/10	Original Teddy, Cinnamon, mhr, LE							38	38			82	111
0214/10	Original Teddy, Gold, mhr, LE							38	38			82	111
0215/35	Dormy Bear	60	67	68	68							150	168
0217/34	Dorma Bear		65	66	66	66	66	70				145	162
0218/14	Gieng-Ling Panda, Hobby Center Toys, LE 1000, 1988 **U**												400
0218/16	Bear		28	28	28	28						60	67
0220/30	Orsi Bear	48	54	55	55							120	150
0223/20	Bruno Bear, Jointed, mhr, LE **U**			60	60	62	62	62				135	250
0224/35	Petsy Soft											93	104
0225/27	Baby Ophelia with Tutu, mhr, LE, 1988 **U**									140	140	140	200
0225/42	Ophelia Bear, Jointed, mhr, LE, 1984 **U**					150	159	169	1100	275	275	275	395
0226/28	Growling Bear										100		135
0227/33	Schnuffy Bear Dressed, 1907 Rep, mhr, LE, 1987 **U**							1100	275	275			379
0228/33	Growling Bear, mhr							90	125	125	125	125	169
0228/38	Growling Bear, mhr							125	165	165	165	165	223
0228/48	Growling Bear, mhr							195	250	250	250	250	338
0230/20	Teddy Petsy, Rust					39	39					69	77
0230/28	Teddy Petsy, Rust					50	50	53	64	95	95	63	71
0230/35	Teddy Petsy, Rust					70	70	75	90	130	130	85	95
0230/45	Teddy Petsy, Rust					100	100	105	140	190	190	120	134
0233/20	Teddy Petsy, Blonde					39	39	41	41			65	73
0233/28	Teddy Petsy, Blonde					50	50	53	65	95	95	63	71

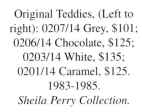

Original Teddies, (Left to right): 0207/14 Grey, $101; 0206/14 Chocolate, $125; 0203/14 White, $135; 0201/14 Caramel, $125. 1983-1985. *Sheila Perry Collection.*

TEDDY BEARS – NUMERICAL

Steiff #	Description	1980-1981	1981-1982	1982-1983	1983-1984	1984-1985	1985-1986	1986	1987	1988	1989	1990	Current
0233/35	Teddy Petsy, Blonde					70	70	75	90	130	130	85	95
0233/45	Teddy Petsy, Blonde					100	100	105	140	190	190	120	134
0233/80	Teddy Petsy, Blonde						400	425	4100	4100		600	672
0235/20	Teddy Petsy, Cream					39	39	41	41			65	73
0235/28	Teddy Petsy, Cream					50	50	53	65	95	95	63	71
0235/35	Teddy Petsy, Cream					70	70	75	90	130	130	85	95
0235/45	Teddy Petsy, Cream					100	100	105	140	190	190	120	134
0236/28	Petsy Teddy, Augbergine											62	69
0237/20	S-Soft Teddy, Beige, Jointed, mhr, LE					40						90	101
0237/28	Petsy Teddy, Blackberry											62	140
0237/28	S-Soft Teddy, Beige, Jointed, mhr, LE					55	59	62	62			125	140
0237/35	S-Soft Teddy, Beige, Jointed, mhr, LE					75	79	85	85			165	185
0237/45	S-Soft Teddy, Beige, Jointed, mhr, LE					110	115	115	115			245	274
0238/35	Petsy Teddy											85	95

Clifford Berryman Bear, 0255/35, LE 1987-1989, $300.

TEDDY BEARS – NUMERICAL

Steiff #	Description	1980-1981	1981-1982	1982-1983	1983-1984	1984-1985	1985-1986	1986	1987	1988	1989	1990	Current
0240/28	Petsy Panda							60	72	110	110	68	76
0240/35	Petsy Panda							80	96	150	150	150	168
0240/45	Petsy Panda							115	140	200		200	224
0243/32	Gold Bear w/Red Ribbon, mhr, WDW, LE 1000, only 500 produced, 1988 **U**									95			750
0244/35	Petsy Bear, White, WDW, LE, 1000, 1989 **U**										115		500
0245/32	Margaret Strong Bear, Grey mhr, WDW, LE 1000, 1990 **U**											125	400
0245/40	Passport Bear, mhr, LE, 1985 **W**						110	115	140	210		225	304
0245/60	Margaret Strong Bear, WDW, LE 10, 1989 **U**												N/P
0245/80	Margaret Strong Bear, WDW, LE 1, 1989 **U**												N/P
0245/80	Petsy, 80cm, WDW, LE 1, 1990 **U**												N/P
0245/99	Petsy, 99cm, WDW, LE 1, 1990 **U**												N/P
0246/32	Mickey Bear, 32 cm, WDW, LE 1500, 1991 **U**												650
0246/60	Mickey Bear, WDW, LE 20, 1991 **U**												3000
0246/80	Mickey Bear, WDW, LE 1, 1991 **U**												N/P
0246/80	Teddy Baby, Charcoal, WDW, LE 1, 1990 **U**											10350	N/P
0246/99	Mickey Bear, WDW, LE 1, 1991 **U**												N/P
0251/34	Berlin Bear, mhr, LE, 1985 **U**						110	115	115			210	275

Teddy Rose, 0171/25,
LE 8000, 1990, $275.

Key: **W = World Wide**
U = USA
E = England
G = Germany
WDW = Walt Disney World
DL = Disneyland
N/P = No prices available

TEDDY BEARS – NUMERICAL

Steiff #	Description	1980-1981	1981-1982	1982-1983	1983-1984	1984-1985	1985-1986	1986	1987	1988	1989	1990	Current
0255/35	Clifford Berryman Bear, mhr, LE								170	225	225		300
0260/25	Jackie Bear Rose, Doll House Southern Bear, LE 1000, 1990 **U**												273
0270/28	Teddy Bear Bride, 1986 **W**							100	125	175		180	202
027062	Preppy Bear 35, Polo, Ralph Lauren, NY, 1994 **U**												350
027079	Chairman II Bear 43, Polo, Ralph Lauren, NY, 1994, LE 1,500 **U**												800
027086	Varsity Bear 35, Polo, Ralph Lauren, NY, 1994, LE 3,500 **U**												350
027093	Producer Bear 43, Polo, Ralph Lauren, NY, 1994, LE 1500 **U**												800
0271/28	Teddy Bear Groom, 1986 **W**							100	125			180	202
0275/28	Teddy/Dr							100	125	175		175	196
0276/28	Teddy Bear with Dirndl, 1986 **W**												225
0276/28	Teddy Dressed with Lederhosen, mhr, 1986 **W**							100	125	175	175	175	196
0277/28	Hans, Marshall Fields, 1985 **U**												300
0278/28	Helga, Marshall Fields, 1985 **U**												300
0280/28	Teddy Dressed as a Sailor Boy, mhr, 1986 **W**							100	125	175	175	175	196
0281/28	Teddy Dressed as a Sailor Girl, mhr, 1986 **W**							100	125	175	175	175	196
0283/28	Teddy Dressed w/Black Forest Outfit, mhr, 1987 **W**								150	150		165	185
0284/28	Teddy Dressed w/Farmer Outfit, mhr, 1987 **W**								150	150		165	185
0285/29	Golden Gate Bear, FAO Schwarz/San Francisco, LE 2000, 1989 **U**												600
0290/32	Toddel	43	50	51								100	112

Petsy, 0181/35, 1927 Replica,
LE 50,000, 1989-1990, $395.
Sheila Perry Collection.

Key: **W** = World Wide
U = USA
E = England
G = Germany
WDW = Walt Disney World
DL = Disneyland
N/P = No prices available

Richard Steiff 1902-1903 Bear,
0150/32, LE, 1983-1985, $164.
Sheila Perry Collection.

Rose Red Teddy Baby, 0128/34, 1987.
Sheila Perry Collection.

Black Bear, 0173/40, 1907 Replica, Prototype, LE
4000, 1988-1989, $800. *Sheila Perry Collection.*

TEDDY BEARS – NUMERICAL

Steiff #	Description	1980-1981	1981-1982	1982-1983	1983-1984	1984-1985	1985-1986	1986	1987	1988	1989	1990	Current
0291/26	Harrods Musical Bear 1909, LE 2000, 1989 **E**												375
0293/32	California Musical Honey Bear, LE 2000, 1989 **U**												275
0294/42	Harrods Musical Bear 1920, Elise von Beethoven, LE 2000, 1991 **E**												N/P
0296/38	Hamleys Tobias mit musikwerk, LE 2000, 1992 **E**												350
0302/30	Zotty	60	67	70	70	70	70					110	123
0302/40	Zotty	85	95	98	98	98	98					160	179
0302/50	Zotty	125	140	145	145	145	145	155				230	258
0305/22	Zotty	34	40	41								200	224
0305/30	Zotty Bear						63	67	81	135	135	85	95
0305/32	Zotty, mhr	46	50	55								270	302
0305/40	Zotty Bear						95	100	125	200	200	125	140
0305/45	Zotty, mhr	98	115	120								410	459
0305/50	Zotty Bear						130	140	170	250	250	150	168
0310/19	Buddha Bear, mhr				40	40	43					130	195
0312/30	Minky Zotty									135	135	89	100
0312/40	Minky Zotty									200	200	130	151
0312/50	Minky Zotty									250	250	155	174
0318/32	Molly Minky										115	77	86
0318/42	Molly Minky										160	160	179
0320/55	Molly Teddy		115	120								230	258
0320/65	Molly Teddy		160	165	165	165	165	175	210	265	265	165	200

Teddy Baby, 0178/32, 1931 Replica, LE, 1990. In 1991 the Steiff tag number changed. For instance this bear for 1991 was tagged 408144.

Key: **W** = World Wide
U = USA
E = England
G = Germany
WDW = Walt Disney World
DL = Disneyland
N/P = No prices available

Steiff #	Description	1980-1981	1981-1982	1982-1983	1983-1984	1984-1985	1985-1986	1986	1987	1988	1989	1990	Current
0321/22	Molly Teddy, Champagne									65	65	42	47
0321/32	Molly Teddy, Champagne									115	115	70	78
0321/55	Molly Teddy, Champagne			100	100	100	105		140	200	200	125	140
0322/22	Molly Teddy, Cream									65	65	42	47
0322/32	Molly Teddy, Cream									115	115	70	78
0322/40	Molly Teddy, Cream					80	80	85	110	150	150	96	108
0323/50	Super Molly Teddy, Standing								395	525		539	604
0323/60	Molly Teddy, Brown											175	196
0323/65	Molly Panda		158	165	165							295	330
0324/60	Super Molly Teddy, Lying								395	525		525	588
0324/75	Molly Teddy											265	297
0326/32	Molly Panda, B/W	52	58	60	60	60	60	65	78	110	110	110	123
0326/45	Molly Panda, B/W	93	100	110	110	110	110	115	140	190		190	213
0327/32	Molly Panda, Brown	48	54									130	146
0327/45	Molly Panda, Brown	90	100									220	246
0327/85	Standing Bear on 4 Legs								2963		4335	3895	4362
0328/99	Bear Standing on 2 Legs								2963		4335	3895	4362
0329/08	Brown Bear Standing on 4 Legs								2315			2500	3200
0329/16	Brown Bear Standing								2315			2500	3200
0330/32	Molly Bear	36	40	41	41	45	45	48	58	95	95	95	106
0330/45	Molly Bear	84	97	100	100	100	100	105	125	160		175	196
0330/70	Molly Bear	190	250	265	265	265						410	459
0331/22	Molly Koala	37	40									76	85
0331/33	Molly Bear, Sitting									185	185	185	207
0331/40	Molly Koala	68	68									125	140
0332/45	Molly Petsy		95	98	98	98						180	202
0333/35	Molly Grizzly		95	98	98							180	202
0334/45	Molly Polar Bear		95	98	98							180	202

Somersault Teddy, 0164/29,
1909 Replica, LE 5000,
1990, $475.
Sheila Perry Collection.

White Bear with Leather Paws, L.E., 1985-1987. (Left) 0158/41, $1000. (Middle Front) 0158/25, $400. (Right) 0158/31, $600.

TEDDY BEARS – NUMERICAL

Steiff #	Description	1980-1981	1981-1982	1982-1983	1983-1984	1984-1985	1985-1986	1986	1987	1988	1989	1990	Current
0334/55	Molly Polar Bear		140	145								270	302
0341/40	Super Molly Bear				90	90	90	95	125	170	170	170	190
0341/65	Super Molly Bear				185	185	185	195	250	350	350	350	392
0341/90	Super Molly Bear				300	300	300	320	400	600	600	600	672
0341/98	Super Molly Bear				450	450	450	475	575			785	879
0341/99	Super Molly Bear	600	680	700	700							920	1030
0343/25	Molly Bear										150	97	109
0343/32	Molly Bear										220	145	498
0343/40	Molly Bear										325	205	230
0345/35	Molly Bear										205	135	151
0345/45	Molly Bear										290	185	207
0345/60	Molly Bear										350	230	258
0345/80	Molly Bear										575	375	420
0347/55	Molly Bear, Brown											165	185
0355/35	Molly Polar Bear, Sitting											135	151
0380/28	Baloo Bear	46	51									225	252
0409/19	Bear, Standing St 69"	2493	2593									4700	5264
0410/50	Bear on Wheels	200										685	1201
0417/60	Brown Bear Cub		175	180	180							340	381
0438/70	Super Molly Panda							195	205	250		320	358

Dicky Bear
(Left) 407550,
1930 Replica,
LE 9000, 1992.
(Right) 0172/32,
1930 Replica, yellow tag,
1985, $650.
Sheila Perry Collection.

Key: W = World Wide
U = USA
E = England
G = Germany
WDW = Walt Disney World
DL = Disneyland
N/P = No prices available

Steiff #	Description	1980-1981	1981-1982	1982-1983	1983-1984	1984-1985	1985-1986	1986	1987	1988	1989	1990	Current
0438/98	Super Molly Panda						425	450	450			695	778
0439/07	Panda					150							600
0439/13	Panda					425							1300
0467/23	Polar Bear, White	50	57	58								95	106
0468/60	Polar Bear Cub		175	180	180							340	381
0470/99	Polar Bear			2565	2565							4600	5152
0472/99	Polar Bear			945	945	945	945	1195			1843	1700	1904
0477/60	Panda Bear Cub		188	195	195							345	386
1210/25	Bear, Standing											81	91
1212/25	Bear, Sitting											89	100
1215/25	Bear, Lying											89	100
1220/25	Polar Bear, Standing											81	91
1222/25	Polar Bear, Sitting											89	100
1225/25	Polar Bear, Lying											89	100
1232/25	Mohair Soft Schwarzbear (Black Bear Cup), FAO Schwarz, LE 2000, 1990 U												250
1444/12	Browny Bear						23	24	30	50	50	32	36
1445/12	Browny Bear	17	20	21	23	29						42	47
1446/11	Koala Bear		22	23	23	23	23	25	30	42	42	45	50
1447/17	Polar Bear		25	26	26							50	56
2877/30	Jr. Petsy			74	74	74						130	146
2920/16	Snuffy Bear				29	29	29	31	38			50	56
2921/16	Snuffy Bear								42	56		60	67
3490/45	Mimic Bear				75	75	75	79	95			165	185
406225	American Flag Bear 35cm, Polo, Ralph Lauren, NY, LE 3,500, 1992 U												425

1907 Teddy Bear, 406034,
Japanese Edition, LE
5000, 1991-1992.
Sheila Perry Collection.

Key: W = World Wide
U = USA
E = England
G = Germany
WDW = Walt Disney World
DL = Disneyland
N/P = No prices available

TEDDY BEARS – NUMERICAL

Steiff #	Description	1980-1981	1981-1982	1982-1983	1983-1984	1984-1985	1985-1986	1986	1987	1988	1989	1990	Current
420016	Teddy Baby Blue, Steiff Club, LE 7959, 1992 **G**												650
420023	Teddy Clown 1928 Club Edition **W**												400
420047	Original Steiff Teddybar 1908 Steiff Aug 1994 Worldwide Steiff Club												N/P
420801	Sam 28, Steiff Club, LE 4000, 1993/94 **U**												750
5030/17	Pummy Bear										90	90	101
5030/21	Pummy Bear										115	115	129
5035/17	Pummy Koala Bear										105	105	118
5035/21	Pummy Koala Bear										140	80	90
5352/33	Cosy Bear									110		110	123
5353/25	Cosy Bear, Honey Gold			53	53							95	106
5354/25	Cosy Bear, Dk. Brown			53	53							65	73
5355/26	Cosy Bear	35	35	35	35	35	35	37	45			95	106
5355/36	Cosy Bear	55	55	55	55	55	55	58	70			95	106
5357/25	Cosy Panda					67	67	70	90	120		120	134
5358/18	Cosy Koala							45	55	80		80	90
5358/27	Cosy Koala			58	58	58	58					95	106
5358/28	Cosy Koala							70	85	125		125	140
5358/38	Cosy Koala							100	125			160	179
5358/50	Cosy Koala							200	250			320	358
5405/17	Cosy Polar Bear					35	35	37	47	47		47	53
5405/30	Cosy Polar Bear				50	50	50	53	64	95	95	95	106
5505/25	Cuddly Bear			50	50							95	106
5600/18	Floppy Bear				36	36	36	38	48	65		65	73
5600/25	Floppy Bear				50	50	50					95	106

Schnuffy 0227/33, 1986, $379. Ophelia, 0225/42, 1987, $395. Baby Ophelia, 0225/27, 1988, $200. *Sheila Perry Collection.*

Steiff #	Description	1980-1981	1981-1982	1982-1983	1983-1984	1984-1985	1985-1986	1986	1987	1988	1989	1990	Current
5651/16	Mini Floppy Bear										50	50	56
5652/16	Min Floppy Polar Bear										50	50	56
5700/20	Teddy	39	43	43								85	95
5700/30	Teddy	57	62	62								120	134
5701/22	Kiddi Bear										75	75	84
5702/20	Kiddi Bear										75	75	84
5750/22	Drolly Bear											52	58
600393	Martini Bear, Polo, Ralph Lauren, NY, 1994, LE 1500 **U**												800
610158	(2) Steiff Bears plus Steiff Teddy Baren Book												750
6242/20	Toldi Bear			25	28							48	54
6242/30	Toldi Bear			49	53	53						90	101
6270/27	Toldi Bear									80		80	90
6360/12	Teddy Shoulder Bag	10	11	12	12							22	25
6361/12	Teddy Coin Purse	10	11	12								22	25
6365/26	Teddy Shoulder Bag, Lg.	17	19	19	19							34	38
6370/22	Bear Music Box	49	54	54	54	54	54	54				97	109
6461/27	Bear (Hand Puppet)	26	28	28	28	28	28	30	36			60	67
6485/32	Happy Bear										95	95	106
650529	Teddy Baby Ticket Seller, LE 5000, 1991 **U**												195
650550	Bear Back Rider Set, LE 5000, 1991 **U**												300
650581	Wellington Bear, Polo, Ralph Lauren, NY, 1994, LE 1500 **U**												450

Molly Braunbär, 0345/80,
yellow tag, $420.
Sheila Perry Collection.

TEDDY BEARS – NUMERICAL

Steiff #	Description	1980-1981	1981-1982	1982-1983	1983-1984	1984-1985	1985-1986	1986	1987	1988	1989	1990	Current
650581	Russia Bear, Polo, Ralph Lauren, NY, 1994, LE 1500 **U**												350
650680	Harrods Musical Bear 1906, LE 2,000, 1993 **U**												400
650918	Original Teddy Bar 36, Spielzeug Ring, Baumwoll-sack, Germany, LE 3000 **W**												N/P
650925	Teddy Bar Eddi 27, Spiel & Spass, Baumwollsack, Germany, LE 2,000 **G**												N/P
651205	Teddy Donald, 30cm, WDW, LE 1500, 1993 **U**												550
651212	Teddy Donald, 60cm WDW, LE 25, 1993 **U**												3000
651243	Winnie the Pooh, 30cm, WDW, LE 2500, 1994 **U**												700
651250	Winnie the Pooh, 60cm, WDW, LE 25, 1994 **U**												N/P
651270	Winnie the Pooh, 80cm, WDW, LE, 1994 **U**												N/P
651526	Teddy Bear, 30cm, Blond, DL, LE 1500, 1993 **U**												400
651533	Teddy Bear. 60cm, Blond, DL, LE 25, 1993 **U**												N/P
651540	Teddy Bear, 80cm, Blond, DL, LE 5, 1993 **U**												N/P
651847	Petsile, The Toy Store, LE 1000, 1993 **U**												195
651854	T.R. The Toy Store, LE 1,500, 1994 **U**												300
651861	Golli G & Teddi B, The Toy Store, LE 1500, 1995												400
652080	Musikteddy 33, FAO Schwarz, LE 2000, 1993 **U**												350
6560/17	Teddy (Hand Puppet)											110	140
6692/30	Bear (Hand Puppet)											85	95
6992/30	Bear (Hand Puppet)	46	50	51	51	51	51	54	65			85	95
7492/05	Pitty Bear	6	7									15	17
7580/27	Toldi Bear SOS										82	82	92
8010/40	Riding Bear	185										355	398
8130/50	Riding Animal, Rocking Bear			285	295	295	295	310	375	600	600	385	600
8150/40	Riding Animal, Riding Bear Rocker		205	210	215	285	285	300				395	442
8155/50	Riding Animal, Bear on Wheels		285	290	295							565	632
8452/22	Nimrod Bear, Caramel, Broken Set, LE					45						100	135
8453/22	Nimrod Bear, White, Broken Set, LE					45	35					96	135
8455/22	Nimrod Bear, Brass, Broken Set, LE					45						100	135
8470/17	Teeny Teddy Bag								60	77		80	90
8472/17	Teeny Bag Panda								60	55		60	67
8490/12	Teddy Minibag					12	12	12	15	22	22	23	25
8492/26	Teddy Bag					19	19	20	24	35		37	41
8494/03	Teddy Pin with Ribbon, mhr							20	19	19		22	25
8495/03	Teddy Pin, Beige, mhr					17	18	19	19			24	27
8496/03	Teddy Pin, Caramel, mhr					17	18	19	19			24	27
8497/03	Teddy Pin, White, mhr					17	18	19	19	19		24	27
8498/03	Teddy Pin, Chocolate, mhr					17	18	19	19	19		24	27
8500/03	Teddy Bear Pin					9	9	10	12	12		14	16
8501/02	Gold Plated Bar Pin w/Jointed Bear								15	18	27	22	25
8505/01	Gold Plated Teddy Earrings						20	21	27	46	46	46	52
8510/02	Gold Plated Teddy Necklace						15	15	16	20	32	32	210	33
999765	Amelia, (with fliers coat/hat/goggles), I. Magnin, LE 650, 1993 **U**												600

Key: W = World Wide • U = USA • E = England • G = Germany • WDW = Walt Disney World • DL = Disneyland • N/P = No prices available

(Left to right) Crocodile Bandsman with Trumpet, 0124/19, $200; cat Bandsman with Drun, 0122/19, $200; Bear Band Leader with Baton, 0120/19, $195; Dog Bandsman with Trombone, 0121/19, $200; Lion Bandsman with Tuba, 0123/29, $200. LE, 1988-1989.

STEIFF SPECIALS

Steiff #	Description	1980-1981	1981-1982	1982-1983	1983-1984	1984-1985	1985-1986	1986	1987	1988	1989	1990	Current
0050/28	Dinosaur, 1959, LE 4000											200	270
0100/86	Elephant on Wheels w/Circus Calp., LE							2100	2100	2100		1200	1200
0100/87	Circus Cage w/Lying Lion, LE									275		550	325
0100/88	Circus Wagon w/Giraffe, LE										325	450	350
0100/89	Circus Wagon w/Tiger, LE										350	550	375
0100/90	Circus Wagon w/Two Bears, LE											450	475
0118/00	Sleigh Set, mhr, LE 6000, 1989 U										275	275	350
0121/19	Dog w/Trombone, LE								125		125	135	200
0130/17	Unicorn, Lying, LE 2000				40	42						135	160
0130/27	Unicorn, Lying, LE 2000				55	57						175	195
0144/19	Gorilla Strong Man, mhr, LE 5000											125	169
0145/19	Elephant Balloon Seller, mhr, LE										135	135	182
0146/19	Hippo Fat Lady, mhr, LE										135	135	182
0147/12	Seal w/Ball, Stand, mhr, LE										100	100	145
0148/03	Teddy Bear Pin				9							15	35
0149/19	Fire Eater Dragon, mhr, LE 5000											125	150
0164/31	Circus Dolly Bear/ Yellow, mhr, LE 2000 white tag, 1987 U								135	175	175	185	250
0164/32	Circus Dolly Bear/Green, mhr, LE 2000 white tag, 1987 U								135	175	175	185	250
0164/34	Circus Dolly Bear/Violet, mhr, LE 2000 white tag, 1987 U								135	175	175	185	250
6360/12	Teddy Shoulder Bag	10	11	12	12							22	25
6361/12	Teddy Coin Purse	10	11	12								22	25
6365/26	Teddy Shoulder Bag, Lg.	17	19	19	19							34	38
6370/22	Bear Music Box	49	54	54	54	54	54	54				97	109
6371/22	Cat Music Box	49										97	109
6376/18	Owl Music Box	44	48	49	49							88	99
6383/18	Ladybug Music Box	26	30									59	66

(Left to Right) Teddy Baby Food Vendor, 0177/19, $175; Gorilla Strongman, 0144/19, $169; Fire Eater Dragon, 0149/19, $150. LE, 1990. *Sheila Perry Collection.*

Key: W = World Wide
U = USA
E = England
G = Germany
WDW = Walt Disney World
DL = Disneyland
N/P = No prices available

71

STEIFF SPECIALS

Circus Wagon Limited Edition Set, *Left to Right:* Circus Wagon with Two Bears, 0100/90, 1990, $475; Circus Wagon with Tiger, 0100/89, 1989, $375; Circus Wagon with Giraffe, 0100/88, 1988, $350.

STEIFF SPECIALS

Circus Wagon Cage with Lying Lion, 0100/87, 1987, $325; Elephant on Wheels with Circus Calliope, 0100/86, 1986, $1200. Limited Editions.

STEIFF SPECIALS

Steiff #	Description	1980-1981	1981-1982	1982-1983	1983-1984	1984-1985	1985-1986	1986	1987	1988	1989	1990	Current
6400/15	Mosaic Ball, Sm., mhr	17	21	22								65	73
6400/20	Mosaic Ball, Med., mhr	28	32	32								110	123
6450/15	Ball				21	21	21	22	27	42		45	50
6450/20	Ball				32	32	32	34	41	65		69	77
8470/17	Teeny Teddy Bag								60	77		80	90
8472/17	Teeny Bag Panda								60	55		60	67
8474/17	Teeny Bag Rabbit								60	55		60	67
8476/17	Teeny Bag Dog								60	55		60	67
8490/12	Teddy Minibag					12	12	12	15	22	22	23	25
8492/26	Teddy Bag					19	19	20	24	35		37	41
8494/03	Teddy Pin with Ribbon, mhr							20	19	19		22	25
8495/03	Teddy Pin, Beige, mhr					17	18	19	19			24	27
8496/03	Teddy Pin, Caramel, mhr					17	18	19	19			24	27
8497/03	Teddy Pin, White, mhr					17	18	19	19	19		24	27
8498/03	Teddy Pin, Chocolate, mhr					17	18	19	19	19		24	27
8500/03	Teddy Bear Pin					9	9	10	12	12		14	16
8501/02	Gold Plated Bar Pin w/Jointed Bear								15	18	27	22	25
8505/01	Gold Plated Teddy Earrings						20	21	27	46	46	46	52
8510/02	Gold Plated Teddy Necklace					15	15	16	20	32	32	210	33
8550/02	Reg Edition, History of Steiff										100	100	112
8601/06	Porcelain Tea Set, 7 pc.									18	15	20	22
8605/01	Wall Plate										9	9	15
8605/06	Mini Tea Set										15	15	40
8605/15	Deluxe Tea Set										57	57	60

(Left to Right) Baby Elephant Balloon Seller, 0145/19, $182; Chimp on Unicycle, 0143/19, $169; Teddy Baby Ringmaster, 0175/19, $200; Seal with Ball, 0147/12, $145; Hippo Fat Lady, 0146/19, $182. LE, 1989. *Sheila Perry Collection.*

RABBITS

RABBITS

Steiff #	Description	1980-1981	1981-1982	1982-1983	1983-1984	1984-1985	1985-1986	1986	1987	1988	1989	1990	Current
0095/17	Begging Rabbit 7x Jntd 1911, LE 4000									145	145	145	196
0134/22	Niki Rabbit, mhr					58						155	209
0134/28	Niki Rabbit, mhr					70		75				195	263
0135/00	Hoppy Rabbit Set, 3 Pieces, 1984 **U**				265								358
0147/20	Rabbit, Begging									50	50	50	68
0155/00	Hoppy Rabbit Set, 3pc. 1984, LE					150	150	150				265	358
0338/34	Molly Rabbit		69	70	70	70						125	140
1350/10	Timmy Rabbit, Mini-Mohair										50	50	55
1350/12	Timmy Rabbit, Mini-Mohair										70	70	78
1500/09	Hoppy, Lying, Brown	14	17	18	18							32	36
1500/13	Hoppy, Beige					25	25	27	33			35	39
1501/09	Hoppy, Lying, Grey	14	17	18	18							32	36
1501/13	Hoppy, Grey					25	25	27	33			35	39
1502/10	Manni, Sitting, Brown	14	17									32	36
1502/15	Manni, Beige					25	25	27	33			35	39
1503/10	Manni, Sitting, Grey	14	17									45	50
1503/15	Manni, Grey					25	25	27	33			35	39
2882/25	Jr. Rabbit, Lying	38	38									75	84
2882/35	Jr. Rabbit, Lying		57	57									110
2910/12	Snuffy Rabbit, Brown	15	19	19								32	36
2910/18	Snuffy Rabbit, Brown	19	24	24								38	43
2911/12	Snuffy Rabbit, Grey	15	19	19								32	36
2911/18	Snuffy Rabbit, Grey	19	24	24								38	43
2931/16	Snuffy, Beige/White				29	29	29	30	38	55		55	62
2932/16	Snuffy, Caramel				29	29	29	30	38	55		55	62

Hoppy Rabbit
Set, 0155/00,
3 pieces, LE,
1984, $358.

Key:
W = World Wide
U = USA
E = England
G = Germany
**WDW = Walt
Disney World**
DL = Disneyland
**N/P = No prices
available**

RABBITS

Steiff #	Description	1980-1981	1981-1982	1982-1983	1983-1984	1984-1985	1985-1986	1986	1987	1988	1989	1990	Current
2933/16	Snuffy, Dark Brown				29	29	29	30	38	55		55	62
2945/25	Rabbit	37	47	48								70	78
2947/35	Ossi, Standing	38	42									70	78
2950/32	Mummy Rabbit, Begging, Beige									120	125	125	140
2955/18	Winni, Grey, Sitting	30	33									60	67
2955/32	Mummy Rabbit, Begging, Grey									120	125	125	140
2956/16	Hoppel Rabbit											37	41
2956/18	Winni, Brown, Sitting	30	33									60	67
2957/13	Hoppel, Grey	33	37	37	37							62	69
2957/22	Hoppel Rabbit											63	71
2958/13	Poppel, Beige	33	37	37	37							62	69
2958/25	Hoppel Rabbit											63	71
2960/22	Sonny, Grey	45	50	51	51	51	51	54	65			86	96
2961/22	Ronny, Beige	45	50	51	51	51	51	54	65			86	96
2962/16	Mummy, Grey	32	35	36	36							61	68
2962/25	Poppel Rabbit											63	71
2963/16	Pummy, Beige	32	35	36	36							60	67
2965/20	Rabbit, Sitting	29	35	35								46	52
2965/25	Rabbit, Sitting	38	50									70	78
2968/35	Snobby Rabbit				72	72	72	76	95			120	134
2970/23	B/W, Sp	43	51	52	52	52						85	90
2970/30	B/W, Spotted	72	89	90	90							150	168
2972/40	Dormy Rabbit, Lying								165	175		110	123
2974/16	Dormili Rabbit							35	50	73	75	47	53
2975/25	Dormy Rabbit						67	71	86	120	125	75	84
2977/20	Dormili Rabbit							37	50	75		75	84
2978/35	Dormy Rabbit, Begging							115	160	165	165		185
2982/17	B/W Spottili, Running							55	75	80	80		90
2984/17	B/W Spottili, Sitting							53	73	75	75		84
2985/30	B/W Spotty, Sitting							100	140			140	157
2992/17	Grey & White Spottili, Running							55	75	80		80	90
2994/17	Grey & White Spottili, Sitting							53	73	75		75	84
2995/30	Grey & White Spotty, Sitting							100	140	150		150	168
3020/00	Manni Rabbit Set, 3 pc., 1983, LE						175	175				375	420
3020/10	Manni Rabbit, mhr				35							95	106
3020/30	Manni Rabbit, mhr				75	75	75					175	196
3135/45	Ango	53	65	65								100	112
3141/43	Lulac, Brown, mhr	36	44									135	151
3142/43	Lulac, Grey, mhr	36										135	151
3155/16	Timmy, Brown	23	28	28	28							45	50
3156/16	Timmy, Grey	23	28	28	28							45	50
3480/40	Elbow Puppet-Rabbit, Grey	58	60	61	65	65	65	69	69			100	112
3480/41	Rabbit, White							69	69			115	129
3481/40	Elbow Puppet-Rabbit, Brown	58	60	61	65	65	65	69				110	123
5060/17	Pummy Rabbit										95	60	67
5060/21	Pummy Rabbit										130	83	92
5063/17	Pummy Rabbit										95	95	106
5063/21	Pummy Rabbit										130	130	146
5067/17	Pummy Rabbit										95	95	106
5067/21	Pummy Rabbit										130	130	146
5361/24	Cosy Manni			43	43	43						80	90
5362/24	Cosy Hoppy			43	43	43	43					80	90
5363/16	Cosy Snuffy, Beige			28	28	28	28	30	36			45	50
5364/16	Cosy Snuffy, Caramel			28	28	28	28		36			45	50

Key: W = World Wide • U = USA • E = England • G = Germany • WDW = Walt Disney World • DL = Disneyland • N/P = No prices available

Begging Rabbit, Replica 1911, 0095/17, LE 4000,
1988-1989, $196.

Manni Rabbit Set, 3020/00 set number, 3 pieces, LE,
1985-1987, $420. *Left to Right:* 3020/30, $196;
3020/10cm, $106; 3020/20.

Niki Rabbit, 402159, 1952 Replica, LE 5000, 1992.
Sheila Perry Collection.

RABBITS

Steiff #	Description	1980-1981	1981-1982	1982-1983	1983-1984	1984-1985	1985-1986	1986	1987	1988	1989	1990	Current
5502/13	Cosy Minni, Sitting, Beige/White									42	44	44	49
5503/13	Cosy Minni, Sitting, Brown/Cream									42	44	44	49
5504/13	Cosy Minni, Sitting, Grey/White									42	44	44	49
5505/13	Cosy Minni, Sitting, Black/White									42	44	44	49
5507/15	Manni, Begging, Brown/White									44	46	46	52
5508/15	Manni, Begging, Brown/Cream									44		44	49
5511/18	Cosy Snuffy, Crouching, Beige/White									60		60	67
5512/18	Cosy Snuffy, Crouching, Rust/Beige									60		60	67
5513/16	Cosy Bunny, Aubergine											37	41
5514/16	Cosy Bunny, Blackberry											37	41
5525/25	Rabbit, Brown			50	50	50						92	103
5526/25	Ango, White		50	51	51	51						95	106
5605/18	Floppy Rabbit				36	36	36	38	48	69		69	77
5605/25	Floppy Rabbit				50	50	50		50			85	95
5658/16	Mini Floppy Rabbit										50	50	56
6060/24	Poppy Rabbit, Blond									80		80	90
6060/32	Poppy Rabbit, Blond									130	130		146
6062/24	Poppy Rabbit, Cinnamon									80	52		58
6062/32	Poppy Rabbit, Cinnamon									130	83		92
6067/24	Poppy Rabbit, Grey									80	80		90
6067/32	Poppy Rabbit, Grey									130	130		146
6235/30	Rabbit	40	40									70	78
6235/40	Rabbit	54	54									92	103
6280/40	Dangling Rabbit		52									90	101
6281/25	Lulac, Grey					43	43	46	57	80	83	55	62
6281/75	Lulac, Grey								200	300	300	195	218
6282/25	Lulac, Beige					43	43	46	57	80	83	55	62
6282/75	Lulac, Brown								200	300	300	300	336
6283/50	Lulac, Brown				72	72	72	76	92	130	135	86	151
6284/99	Lulac, Cream										575	575	644
6463/27	Rabbit (Hand Puppet)	30	33	33	33	33	33	35	42			55	62
6490/32	Happy Rabbit										105	105	118
6600/17	Rabbit (Hand Puppet), mhr	20										85	95
6993/30	Rabbit (Hand Puppet)	46	50	51	51	51	51	54	65			85	95
7010/45	Grey Jolly Rabbit Elbow Puppet									170		175	196
7136/04	Rabbits, Assmt	5	7	7	7	7						11	12
7146/06	Rabbits, Assmt	8	10	10	10	10	10	10	12			15	17
7156/08	Rabbits, Assmt	13	15	15	15	15	15	16	20			22	25
7495/05	Pitty Rabbit	6	7		7	7	7					10	12

CATS

(Left) Drink Cat, 0108/14, Replica 1933, LE 4000, 1990, $250. *(Right)* Kitty Cat, 1307/12, 1990, $78.

CATS

Steiff #	Description	1980-1981	1981-1982	1982-1983	1983-1984	1984-1985	1985-1986	1986	1987	1988	1989	1990	Current
0104/10	Tabby Cat, 1928 Rep., LE 6000							75	75	120		130	176
0108/14	Drinking Cat, 1933, LE 4000											185	250
0122/19	Cat W/Drum, LE									125	125	135	200
0146/13	Cat, Crouching								50	50	50	50	68
0334/33	Molly Cat										175	175	196
1307/12	Kitty Cat, White, mhr											70	78
1314/12	Cat Kitty, Black, mhr											70	78
1493/13	Susi Cat, Grey			23	23	23	23	25	30	45		45	50
1493/14	Cat, Black			23	23	23						45	50
1495/10	Kitty Cat	14	16	17								39	44
1496/10	Black Tom Cat	22	24	25	25	25						52	58
2710/28	Cat Minka, Standing											92	103
2715/35	Cat Minka, Lying											84	94
2720/22	Cat, Grey	37	37									70	78
2725/22	Cat, Spotted	37	45									70	78
2726/17	Sissi Cat	35	38	39	39	39	39	41	50	75	75	47	53
2726/22	Sissi Cat	45	49	50	50	50	50	53	65	95		95	106
2728/17	Lizzy Cat	35	38	39	39	39	39	41	50	75	75	75	84
2728/22	Lizzy Cat	45	49	50	50	50	50	53	65	95		95	106
2732/17	Tabby	35	38	39	39							75	84
2735/16	Sulla Cat, Cream					38	38	40				75	84
2735/26	Sulla Cat, Cream					58	58	61				105	118
2736/16	Sulla Cat, Grey					38	38	40	48	75		75	84
2736/26	Sulla Cat, Grey					58	58	61	75	105		105	118
2738/16	Dossy Cat, Black					38	38	40	48	75	75	75	84
2738/26	Dossy Cat, Black					58	58	61	75	105	105	105	118
2740/25	Siamese		57	63	64	64							120
2742/23	Cat									120	120	200	224
2745/30	Cat, Lying				75	75						130	146
2750/22	Ringel Cat, Lying		50	50	50							90	101
2752/26	Persian Cat, Grey			62	63	63	63					110	123
2752/35	Persian Cat, Grey			110	110	110						195	218
2753/26	Angora Cat, White			62	63	63	63					110	123
2754/25	Minou Cat, Lying, Cream							70	85	120	120	120	134
2754/40	Minou Cat, Lying, Cream							100	125	175	175	120	134
2755/25	Minou Cat, Lying, Grey							70	85	120		120	134
2755/40	Minou Cat, Lying, Grey							100	125	175		175	196
2756/25	Minou Cat, Lying, Black							70	85	120	120	120	134
2756/40	Minou Cat, Lying, Black							100	125	175		175	196
2757/25	Minou Cat, Striped								92	120	120	120	134
2757/40	Minou Cat, Striped								130	175	175	175	196
2758/40	Cat									175	175	175	196

Mini Floppy, 5678/16, $59 and Fuzzy Tag, 1464/12, $56. Yellow tag. *Sheila Perry Collection.*

Key: W = World Wide
U = USA
E = England
G = Germany
WDW = Walt Disney World
DL = Disneyland
N/P = No prices available

CATS

Steiff #	Description	1980-1981	1981-1982	1982-1983	1983-1984	1984-1985	1985-1986	1986	1987	1988	1989	1990	Current
2926/16	Snuffy Cat				32	32	32					55	62
2927/16	Snuffy Cat				32	32	32					55	62
2928/16	Snuffy Cat								50	65	65	42	47
3483/40	Elbow Puppet-Cat	70	76									135	151
3520/12	Snuffy Cat, Beige	17	21	22								36	40
3520/17	Snuffy Cat, Beige	22	28									40	45
3521/12	Snuffy Cat, Grey	17	21	22								36	40
3521/17	Snuffy Cat, Grey	22	28	29								40	45
3740/25	Siamese		57	63	64	64							120
5440/16	Cosy Sulla, Cream							40	43	52	52	52	58
5440/22	Cosy Sulla, Cream							50	53	65		65	73
5442/16	Cosy Milla, Blonde							40	43	52		52	58
5442/22	Cosy Milla, Blonde							50	53	65	65	65	73
5520/25	Cat, Grey			50	50	50	50					90	101
5620/18	Floppy Cat				36	36	36	38	48	70		60	67
5620/25	Floppy Cat				50	50	50	53	65	100		100	111
5665/16	Mini Floppy Cat										50	50	56
5717/20	Kiddi Cat										75	75	84
5720/20	Cat	39	43									69	77
5720/30	Cat	57	62									100	112
5780/22	Drolly Cat											52	58
6080/32	Poppy Cat										135	135	151
6225/28	Possy Cat										115	115	137
6275/27	Toldi Cat									90		90	101
6285/60	Dangling Tomcat	105										185	207
6290/32	Dangling Cat "Burri"							60	72	110		110	123
6466/27	Cat (Hand Puppet)	30	33	33	33							55	62
6494/32	Happy Cat										115	115	129
6660/17	Cat, Grey (Hand Puppet), mhr	20										85	95
6998/30	Cat	46	50									85	95
7494/05	Pitty Cat	6	7									9	10

Mini Floppy,
5665/16, $56;
Sissi, 074103;
Siamy Katze,
400810.
White tag, 1994.
*Sheila Perry
Collection.*

DOGS

DOGS

Steiff #	Description	1980-1981	1981-1982	1982-1983	1983-1984	1984-1985	1985-1986	1986	1987	1988	1989	1990	Current
0101/14	Bully Dog, 1927 Rep, LE 6000							75	75	120		145	225
0118/25	Boxer, Lying, mhr, LE 2000					55	57	57	57	57			85
0332/33	Molly Dog										175	175	196
0337/50	Schnauzer	138	170									270	302
0338/35	Molly Chow	63	76									115	129
0338/60	Molly Chow	145	175									230	258
0340/35	Molly Husky	72	89									115	129
0340/60	Molly Husky	145	175									230	258
0342/40	S-Molly St. Bernard					80	80					130	146
0342/60	S-Molly St. Bernard					150	150					245	274
0342/80	S-Molly St. Bernard					275	275	295				450	504
0342/98	S-Molly St. Bernard					400	400	425				660	739
0342/99	Super Molly Dog		680	700	700							1050	1176
0343/50	Molly Bello Dog								185	185		185	207
0350/45	Molly Dog		95	98	98	98						180	202
0350/65	Molly Dog		157	160	160							295	330
0460/45	Molly Husky										195	125	140
0460/60	Molly Husky										330	330	370
1306/12	Waldi Hound, Tan, mhr											70	78
1313/12	Hound Waldi, Brown, mhr											70	78
1526/11	Dog	13	15									34	38
1528/11	Fox Terrier	15	18	19	19	27	27					36	40
1530/12	Schnauzer	17	19									40	45

Bully Dog, 0101/14,
1927 Replica,
Museum Collection,
LE 6000, 1986, $225.
Nadine Gravatt Collection.

Key: W = World Wide
U = USA
E = England
G = Germany
WDW = Walt Disney World
DL = Disneyland
N/P = No prices available

DOGS

Steiff #	Description	1980-1981	1981-1982	1982-1983	1983-1984	1984-1985	1985-1986	1986	1987	1988	1989	1990	Current
1532/12	Poodle, Black	18	20	21	21	21						40	45
1533/12	Poodle, White	18	20	21	21	21						40	45
2882/35	Jr. Fox Terrier			81	89	89	89	95				165	185
2883/30	Jr. Schnauzer, Sitting	67										120	134
2883/35	Jr. Charly Dog			81	81	81	81	86				140	157
2884/26	Jr. Cockie		75	75	75							125	140
2884/30	Jr. Schnauzer, Lying	67										120	134
2885/28	Dog, Sitting	59	70									110	123
2886/28	Dog, Lying	59	70									110	123
2887/26	Swiss Mtn Dog			75	75							140	157
2888/35	St. Bernard	90	110	115	115							170	190
2890/22	Jr. Pekinese			53	53	53	53					95	106
2893/30	Jr. Scotch Terrier			74	74	74						135	151
2923/16	Snuffy Dog				32	32	32	34	42	62		62	69
3492/45	Mimic Dog				75	75	75	79	95			120	134
4010/12	Mopsy Dog, mhr	17	20									75	84
4026/21	Spaniel Cockie, Sitting											74	83
4028/32	Spaniel Cockie, Lying											88	99
4030/14	Pekinese		40	41	41	43	43					75	84
4035/38	Cocker Spaniel					80	80	85	110	150		150	168
4040/99	St. Bernard Dog	450	615	610	665							1065	1193
4045/35	Boxer				80	80	80	85	105	175	175	175	196
4045/50	Boxer, Lying			130	130	130	130	138	165	250	250	105	118
4048/40	German Shepherd				80	80	80					135	151
4048/50	German Shepherd			130	130	130	130	138	165	250		250	280
4050/80	Shepherd, Standing	665	775	796	796							1200	1344
4052/80	Shepherd, Lying	565	625	639	639							1075	1204
4053/20	German Shepherd Puppy				33	33	33					55	62
4053/23	Shepherd, Puppy	66	74	75	75	75	75					125	140
4055/65	Husky	580	650									995	1114
4060/80	Setter, Standing	520	600									1000	1120
4061/80	Setter, Sitting	520	600	602	602							1100	1232
4065/65	Chow	545	600	602	602	585						1000	1120
4070/55	Schnauzer	245	275	285	285							490	549
4075/60	Boxer	500	575	575	745	745						1110	1243
4080/50	Terrier	255	285	285	285	285						490	549
4085/28	Terrier	72	79									135	151

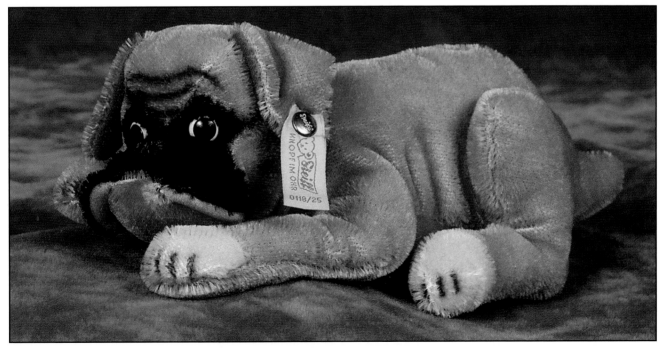

Boxer, 0118/25, LE 2000, $85. *Sheila Perry Collection.*

Dogs

Steiff # Description

Steiff #	Description	1980-1981	1981-1982	1982-1983	1983-1984	1984-1985	1985-1986	1986	1987	1988	1989	1990	Current
4090/40	Collie				80	80	80	85	110			160	179
4121/30	Pomeranian, White	72	80	82	82							135	151
4122/30	Pomeranian, Rust	72	80									135	151
4130/20	Mobby Bobtail Dog, Sitting									80	80	80	90
4132/24	Mobby Bobtail Dog, Standing									125	125	125	140
4140/30	Fox Terrier "Treff"									145	145	92	103
4142/12	Dachshund	24	26	27	27	30	30	32				45	50
4150/25	Raudi Dachshund, Sand/Grey							75	90	135		135	151
4150/40	Raudi Dachshund, Sand/Grey							100	125	190		190	213
4151/25	Raudi Dachshund, Grey/Brown							75	90	135		135	151
4151/40	Raudi Dachshund, Grey/Brown							100	125	190		190	213
4153/25	Dog Raudi											98	110
4156/26	Poodle, Brown	55	60									105	118
4157/26	Poodle, Black	55	60									105	118
4157/50	Poodle, Standing	255	285	285	285							495	554
4158/50	Poodle, Upright	275	300									540	605
4160/24	Welfo Puppy, Standing							95	125		125	125	140
4160/35	Poodle, Black	67	74									120	134
4161/35	Poodle, White	67	74									120	134
4162/22	Welfo Puppy, Lying								100	135		140	157
4162/35	Poodle, Apricot	67	74									120	134
4165/45	Wolfi Dog, Sitting								225	300		320	358
4167/40	Shepherd Dog Arco, Sitting											135	151
4168/45	Shepherd Dog Arco, Lying											170	190
4180/45	Afgan Dog, Standing								235	315		325	364
4182/40	Afgan Dog, Sitting								175	230		245	274
4184/35	Blacky S. Terrier										160	160	179
4185/35	Whity W.H. Terrier										160	160	179
4192/25	Yorkshire Terrier, Sitting								125	165	165	165	185
4215/21	Fox Terrier	48	52									85	95
4215/30	Fox Terrier	73										135	151
5368/33	Cosy Dog								95			95	106
5445/20	Cosy Poodle Tobby, Stndg, Apricot							50	60	90		90	101
5445/28	Cosy Poodle Tobby, Stndg, Apricot							70	87	135		135	151
5447/20	Cosy Poodle Tobby, Stndg, Black							50	60	90		90	101
5447/28	Cosy Poodle Tobby, Stndg, Black							70	87	135		135	151
5452/28	Cosy Poodle Nobby, Lying, Grey							75	90	135		135	151
5457/20	Cosy Dog Bello Standing, Grey							50	60	90		90	101
5457/27	Cosy Bello-Dog					63	63					100	112
5460/35	Cosy Daschund			81	81	81	81					145	162
5463/50	Cosy Basset Dog				125	125		135	165	225		225	252
5465/16	Cosy Lumpi Schnauzer						34	36	44	70		70	78
5465/27	Cosy Lumpi Schnauzer						55	58	71	120		120	134
5466/16	Cosy Lumpi Schnauzer, Lying						36	38	46	75		75	84
5530/25	Cuddly Dog			50	50							90	101
5610/18	Floppy Dog				36	36	38	38	48	70		70	78
5610/25	Floppy Dog				50							85	95
5662/16	Mini Floppy Dog										53	53	59
5712/20	Kiddi Dog										75	75	84
5717/20	Terrier	41	44									75	84
5717/30	Terrier	59	65									100	112
5820/22	Dog	43	48									79	88
6276/27	Toldi Dog									80		80	90
6284/60	Dangling Dog	105	115									185	207
6287/70	Dangling Dog											220	246
6291/32	Dangling Dog "Lumpi"							60	72	110		110	123
6464/27	Dog (Hand Puppet)	30	32									55	62
6640/17	Fox Terrier (Hand Puppet), mhr	20										85	95
6994/30	Dog (Hand Puppet)	46	50									85	95
7497/05	Pitty Dog	6	7									9	10
7690/20	Shepard	31	34									60	67

Key: W = World Wide • U = USA • E = England • G = Germany • WDW = Walt Disney World • DL = Disneyland • N/P = No prices available

FARMYARD ANIMALS

Molly Lamby, 0370/40, 1981-1985, $157.

FARMYARD ANIMALS

Steiff #	Description	1980-1981	1981-1982	1982-1983	1983-1984	1984-1985	1985-1986	1986	1987	1988	1989	1990	Current
0081/14	Felt Duck, 1892 Rep., LE 4000									125	125	125	169
0091/14	Pig, Univ Head Movement, 1909, LE 4000										155	155	225
0126/20	Donkey Mechanical 1909 Rep, LE									185	185	185	250
0145/12	Lamb								30	30		30	41
0333/55	Molly Grizzly		170	175								330	370
0335/55	Molly Donkey		95	98	98	98	98	105	125	175		180	202
0335/80	Molly Donkey	185	250									370	414
0336/55	Molly Pony		95	98								198	222
0360/45	Molly Pig		95	98	98	98	98	105	125	175		180	201
0361/90	Super Molly Pig				275	275	275	295	375	525	525	310	347
0363/40	Molly Zicky Goat											115	129
0363/50	Molly Zicky Goat											150	168
0365/40	Molly Pony, Brown								125		125	77	86
0365/50	Molly Pony								175	235		235	263
0365/99	Super Molly Cow				400	400	400					700	784
0366/99	Super Molly Pony				400	400	400	425				700	784
0367/40	Molly Pony, Black									125		125	140
0367/99	Super Molly Donkey				400	400	400	425	425			700	784
0370/40	Molly Lamb		74	76	76	76						140	157
0440/99	Goat										3550	3000	3360
0445/60	Little Goat										1000	575	644
0446/60	Little Goat										1000	575	644
0450/99	Donkey										3975	3995	4474
0453/75	Little Donkey										2750	2000	2240
1505/10	Piggy Pig		22	23	23	23	23	25	30	45	45	30	33
1510/14	Donkey	17	19	21	23	29	29					45	50
1516/14	Pony	17	20	21	23	17	17	29				34	38
1518/11	Lamb	13	16	17	17	17	17	18	22			40	45
1520/11	Sheep, B/W	13	16	17	17	17	17	18	22			40	45
1522/14	Horse								38	58	58	37	41
1524/12	Cow								38	58	58	58	64
1525/08	Pig								34	50	50	50	56
1526/12	Brown Baby Goat								36	50	55	55	62
1527/12	White Baby Lamb								36	50	55	55	62
1834/40	Lamb	66										120	134
2918/18	Snuffy Pig								50	66	66	66	74
3205/15	Tulla Duck	23	27	28	28	28	28	30	36			43	48
3210/16	Willa Duck, Green									46	48	48	54
3210/22	Willa Duck, Green									60		60	67
3211/16	Pilla Duck, Blue									46		50	56
3211/22	Pilla Duck, Blue									60		60	67
3215/16	Tulla Duck, Red									46		50	56
3215/22	Tulla Duck, Red									60		60	67
3230/11	Duck Daggi										35	35	39
3232/11	Duck Daggi										35	35	39
3240/16	Duck Waggi											35	39
3240/20	Duck Waggi											48	54
3242/08	Piccy Duck	10	11	11								25	28
3242/11	Piccy Duck	14	16	16								32	36
3243/16	Duck Waggi											35	39
3243/20	Duck Waggi											48	54
3450/22	Locky Lamb	36	40									72	81
3455/17	Zicky Goat			38	38	38						70	78
3455/56	Zicky Goat			60	60							100	112

Key: W = World Wide • U = USA • E = England • G = Germany • WDW = Walt Disney World • DL = Disneyland • N/P = No prices available

FARMYARD ANIMALS

Steiff #	Description	1980-1981	1981-1982	1982-1983	1983-1984	1984-1985	1985-1986	1986	1987	1988	1989	1990	Current
3460/20	Rocky Wild Goat			41	43	43						80	90
3460/25	Lamb Lamby										77	77	86
3460/30	Lamb Lamby										95	95	106
3462/22	Lamb Lamby										65	43	48
3464/22	Lamb Lamby, Brown										65	43	48
3605/27	Donkey	39	47									75	84
3710/60	Pony on Wheels	225										675	1181
3750/18	Pony, Brown, mhr	24	29									120	134
3760/25	Horse, Brown	57	63	64	65	65	65					110	112
3785/25	Horse, Beige	53	58	59	59							100	112
3790/18	Calf	34	38	38								65	73
3792/25	Cow	57	63	64	64							110	123
3795/27	Calf, Lying			66	72	72	72	76	93			115	129
3810/17	Pig	34	38	38	38	38	38	40	48	70	70	45	65
5360/25	Cosy Pony			45	46	46	46					85	95
5360/40	Pony	76	83	85	85	85						135	151
5376/11	Preppy Duck, Boy							20	21	28	40	40	45
5376/12	Preppy Duck, Girl							20	21	28	40	40	45
5377/12	Cosy Piccy Duck			17	18	18	18					32	36
5378/17	Cosy Daggi Duck			21	22	22	22	23				39	44
5414/18	Cosy Piggy Pig							30	32	39	63	63	40	45
5415/28	Cosy Pig			49	52	52	52	55	66	100	95	61	68
5447/25	Cosy Flora Cow											125	140
5472/20	Cosy Grissy Donkey							44	53	80	80	80	90
5472/28	Cosy Grissy Donkey					66	66	70	87	87		87	97
5473/25	Cosy Lamby							52	71	110		110	123

(Left) Zicky Goat, 3455/17, 1982-1985, $78. *(Right)* Donkey, 0126/20, Replica 1909, LE, 1988-1990, $250.

FARMYARD ANIMALS

Steiff #	Description	1980-1981	1981-1982	1982-1983	1983-1984	1984-1985	1985-1986	1986	1987	1988	1989	1990	Current
5473/40	Cosy Lamby							72	115	175		175	196
5474/21	Cosy Lamb						39	41	50	70		70	78
5474/27	Cosy Lamb						60	65	78	115		115	129
5475/20	Cosy Horse Ferdy, Brown							44	53	80	80	50	56
5475/28	Cosy Horse Ferdy						59	62	75	125	125	125	140
5476/20	Cosy Horse Yello, Beige							44	53	80		80	90
5480/22	Cosy Zicky Goat								70	100		110	123
5491/18	Gocki Rooster								58	85	85	85	95
5495/18	Gacki Hen								58	85	85	85	95
5498/10	Cosy Bibi Chick								19	27		30	34
5625/18	Floppy Lamb				36	36	36	38	48	65		70	78
5625/25	Floppy Lamb				50	50	50	53	65	95		95	106
5668/16	Mini Floppy Lamb										50	50	56
5672/16	Mini Floppy Donkey										53	53	59
5675/16	Mini Floppy Pig										50	50	56
5725/20	Floppy Lamb			41								75	84
5725/30	Floppy Lamb			59								110	123
6202/14	Friedericke, Yellow Goose									47	49	31	55
6203/26	Friedericke, Yellow Goose, Dressed Grl									80	85	85	95
6205/14	Frederic, White Gander									47	49	31	35
6206/26	Frederic, White Gander									80	85	85	95
6210/20	Cuddly Goose, Yellow										65	65	73
6210/32	Cuddly Goose, Yellow										100	100	112
6212/20	Cuddly Goose, Brown										65	65	73
6212/32	Cuddly Goose, Brown										100	100	112

Zicky, 1526/12, $62; Lamby, 3460/25, $86; Lamby, 3464/22, $48. Yellow tag. *Sheila Perry Collection.*

FARMYARD ANIMALS

Steiff #	Description	1980-1981	1981-1982	1982-1983	1983-1984	1984-1985	1985-1986	1986	1987	1988	1989	1990	Current
6212/50	Cuddly Goose, Brown										200	200	224
6422/24	Donkey Pull Toy			62								115	129
6996/30	Donkey (Hand Puppet)	46										85	95
7212/08	Duckling	9	10									14	16
7240/08	Rooster	7	8	8								11	12
7245/08	Rooster	9	11	11	11							16	18
7250/08	Hen	7	8	8								11	12
7255/08	Hen	9	11	11	11	11						16	18
7260/04	Chick	4	5	6	6							8	9
7260/06	Chick	5	7	7	7	7						10	11
7260/08	Chick	9	11	11	11							16	18
7496/05	Pitty Lamb	6	7									9	10
8020/45	Rocking Duck	150										295	330
8135/50	Riding Animal, Rocking Pony			285	295	295	295	310	375	600	600	385	500
8175/60	Riding Animal, Pony on Wheels		295	300	300							570	638
8195/45	Riding Animal, Rocking Duck		175	180	175	175	175					330	370

(Left to Right) 0737/86, purple; Waggi, 3240/16, yellow, $39; 0737/17, gold;
Waggi, 3243/16, black, tan and white, $39. *Sheila Perry Collection.*

Key: W = World Wide • U = USA • E = England • G = Germany • WDW = Walt Disney World • DL = Disneyland • N/P = No prices available

WOODLAND ANIMALS

Goldy

Steiff
KNOPF IM OHR

WOODLAND ANIMALS

Steiff #	Description	1980-1981	1981-1982	1982-1983	1983-1984	1984-1985	1985-1986	1986	1987	1988	1989	1990	Current
0055/00	Eric Bat Set, 2 pc., 1960, LE 4000											200	270
0093/12	Fox, 1910, LE 4000										150	150	203
0345/25	Molly Woodchuck		43	43	43	43						80	90
0346/30	Molly Groundhog	48	57	58	58	58	58	61	75	115		120	134
0347/55	Fox		148	150	150	150	150	160	195			280	314
0348/22	Molly Raccoon	42	52	53								110	123
1308/12	Mouse Fiep, Grey, mhr											60	67
1310/12	Mouse Fiep, White, mhr											60	67
1311/12	Fox Fuzzy											70	78
1312/12	Possy Squirrel, mhr											70	78
1464/12	Fox Woodland Animal							25	34	50		50	56
1465/10	Fox	19	21	22	22	24	24	26	32			45	50
1466/12	Squirrel Woodland Animal							25	36	50	50	32	36
1467/10	Squirrel	17	19	20	20	20	20					39	44
1470/12	Paddy Beaver		20	21	21	21	21	22	27	40	40	40	45
1476/12	Marmot Woodland Animal							25	34	50	50	50	56
1480/12	Ermine Woodland Animal							25	34			50	56
1540/20	Xorry Fox, Lying							40	48	70	70	46	52
1542/35	Red Fox, Sleeping	67	75	76	76	76	76	80	96	120	120	74	83

Fox, 0093/12, Replica 1910, LE 4000, 1989-1990, $203.

Previous Page: Super Goldy Hamster, 2150/50, 1985-1988, $347.

WOODLAND ANIMALS

Steiff #	Description	1980-1981	1981-1982	1982-1983	1983-1984	1984-1985	1985-1986	1986	1987	1988	1989	1990	Current
1543/35	Raccoon, Sleeping	67	67									175	196
1544/35	Fox, Sleeping, Beige	70	78	79	79							175	196
1548/25	Fuzzy Fox										115	78	87
1550/12	Owl Woodland Animal							25	30	50	50	31	35
1670/06	Hedgehog, Lying, mhr	4	5	5	6	6	6	7	8	14	14	14	15
1670/10	Hedgehog	9	10	13	14	16	16					44	49
1670/17	Hedgehog, Lying, mhr	17	21	23	25	28	28					75	84
1675/12	Joggi Hedgehog						18	19	23	40	40	25	28
1675/18	Joggi Hedgehog						24	25	30	50	50	50	56
1675/35	Hedgehog Joggi											93	104
1675/45	Super Joggi Hedgehog							60	145	220		220	246
1675/70	Super Joggi Hedgehog							295	360	500		500	560
1677/14	Joggi Hedgehog, Begging						24	25	30	50	50	32	36
1677/20	Hedgehog Joggi											46	52
1677/50	Hedgehog									350		350	392
1680/12	Hedgehog, Begging, mhr	16	20	21	22	22	22					70	78
1820/14	Fawn	24	26	27	27							58	65
1830/40	Deer, Standing	85	95	98								155	174
1831/20	Fawn, Lying									75	75	48	54
1831/38	Fawn, Lying	55	63	64	64	64	64	68	82	100	100	100	111

Screech Owl, 2593/28,
1981-1988, $218.

Key: W = World Wide
U = USA
E = England
G = Germany
WDW = Walt Disney World
DL = Disneyland
N/P = No prices available

92

WOODLAND ANIMALS

Steiff #	Description	1980-1981	1981-1982	1982-1983	1983-1984	1984-1985	1985-1986	1986	1987	1988	1989	1990	Current
1835/22	Fawn, Standing									100	100	100	111
1837/30	Doe, Lying									120	120	120	134
1838/30	Roebuck, Standing									145	145	145	162
1840/26	Diggy Badger							60	72	110		115	129
1840/36	Diggy Badger							80	100	150		165	185
2015/24	Squirrel									135	135	86	96
2025/18	Chipmunk Chippy										90	60	67
2030/20	Squirrel	31	37	38						75		58	65
2032/25	Possy Squirrel			41	41	41	41	44				75	84
2040/12	Perri Squirrel, mhr	18	22	23	23							85	95
2040/17	Perri Squirrel, mhr	22										110	123
2042/24	Marmot Piff, Grey/Brown											63	71
2050/25	Raggy Racoon, Standing								95	125	125	81	91
2055/35	Raggy Racoon, Sitting								145	195	195	120	134
2060/20	Raggy Ringel Racoon								65	90	90	57	64

Eric Bat Set, 1960 Replica, 0055/00, LE 4000, 1990, $270.

Steiff #	Description	1980-1981	1981-1982	1982-1983	1983-1984	1984-1985	1985-1986	1986	1987	1988	1989	1990	Current
2070/25	Piff Marmot, Standing								85	110	110	110	123
2080/35	Skunk										160	105	118
2121/18	Beaver	29										55	62
2125/20	Nagy Beaver		34	35	35	35	35	37	37			65	73
2150/12	Goldy Hamster						24	25	30	50		50	56
2150/16	Goldy Hamster						29	31	38	62		65	73
2150/50	Super Goldy Hamster						295	310	310	310		310	347
2155/12	Hamster	17	20	21	21	21						34	38
2155/17	Hamster	22	27	27	27	27						42	47
2170/10	Mouse, White	11	13	14	14	14	14	15	18	30	30	30	34
2171/10	Mouse, Grey	11	13	14	14	14	14	15	18	30	30	30	34
2180/12	Mole/Shovel, mhr	11	14	18	19	19	19	20	24	40		45	50
2180/15	Maxi Mole	22	29	30	30	30	30					45	50
2205/12	Woodchuck	24	26	27	27	27	27					49	55
2252/10	Guinea Pig	19	21	22	22	22	22	23	28	40		42	47
2254/15	Guinea Pig					29	29	31				48	54
2255/15	Guinea Pig, Mama	24	30									49	55
2256/15	Guinea Pig, Papa	24	30	31	31							48	54
2270/22	Mouse Pieps, Grey											66	74
2275/22	Mouse Pieps, White											66	74
2370/08	Frog, Sitting	17	20	21	21	24	24	26	32			39	44
2380/32	Frog, Dangling	29	32	32	32	32						57	64
2455/14	Turtle	19	23	24	24	24						85	95
2455/22	Turtle	36										135	151
2460/30	Ladybug/Wheels, mhr	145										445	498
2580/14	Raven Hucky											45	50
2590/50	Owl		295									475	532
2591/22	Owlet		50	50	50	50	50	53	65	90	90	90	101
2592/25	Baby Owl Wiggy											59	66
2593/28	Screech Owl		97	99	99	99	99	105	125	190		195	218
2603/28	Woodpecker, Spotted	82	82									158	177
2604/28	Woodpecker, Green	82	82									158	177
2622/18	Wittie Eagle Owl								55	75	75	75	84
2622/24	Wittie Eagle Owl								89	120		120	134
2622/40	Pheasant	260	295	295	295							495	554
2623/40	Golden Pheasant	275	300	315	315							550	616
2625/15	Owl	26	30	31	31	31	31	33	40			58	65
2625/25	Owl	41	50	50	50							80	90
2881/35	Fox, Crouching	70	85									140	157
2892/28	Jr. Fuzzy Fox		79	80	80							150	168
2916/16	Snuffy Fox								50	67	67	67	75
3476/40	Elbow Puppet-Skunk	80	87	88								150	168
3477/50	Elbow Puppet-Raccoon	80	87	88								150	168
3515/14	Snuffy Fox	19	24									38	43
3515/18	Snuffy Fox	25	32									50	56
4900/22	Fox	22										42	47
5250/17	Fox Pummy										100	66	74
5250/21	Fox Pummy										135	88	99
5382/43	Cosy Froggy		70									135	151
5384/16	Cosy Froggy Frog							44	53	80	80	52	58
5384/20	Cosy Froggy Frog						44	47	57	57		57	64
5384/28	Cosy Froggy Frog						75	80	96	96		96	108
5384/50	Super Cosy Froggy Frog							325	395	395		445	498
5390/30	Cosy Mouse, Blue		42									80	90

Key: W = World Wide • U = USA • E = England • G = Germany • WDW = Walt Disney World • DL = Disneyland • N/P = No prices available

WOODLAND ANIMALS

Steiff #	Description	1980-1981	1981-1982	1982-1983	1983-1984	1984-1985	1985-1986	1986	1987	1988	1989	1990	Current
5391/30	Cosy Mouse, Violet		42									80	90
5392/15	Cosy Mouse, Olive		22										45
5392/30	Cosy Mouse, Green		42	43	43	43	43					80	90
5393/15	Cosy Mouse, White		22	23	23	23	23					40	45
5393/45	Cosy Fiep Mouse, White								145	190		190	213
5394/15	Cosy Mouse, Grey		22	23	23							40	45
5394/45	Cosy Fiep Mouse, Grey								145	190		190	213
5396/17	Cosy Nagy Beaver							31	40	60	60	60	67
5396/22	Cosy Nagy Beaver							46	65	95		95	106
5397/15	Cosy Hedgehog		20	21	21	21	21					39	44
5397/25	Cosy Joggi Hedgehog		30	30	30	30						55	62
5432/20	Snail "Nelly", Purple								55			55	62
5434/20	Snail Nelly, Brown								55			55	62
5558/10	Mini Cosy Hedgehog							15	18	28	28	28	31
5565/10	Blue Bird								19	30		32	36
5567/10	Brown Bird								19	30		32	36
5678/16	Mini Floppy Fox										53	53	59
5722/20	Kiddi Mouse										75	75	84
5725/20	Kiddi Hedgehog										75	75	84
5728/20	Kiddi Fox										75	75	84
5790/22	Drolly Fox											52	58
6020/32	Poppy Raccoon										135	135	151
6215/30	Fox	40										72	81
6240/28	Possy Fox										120	78	87
6245/28	Possy Hedgehog										115	115	129
6273/27	Toldi Hedgehog									80	80	80	90
6274/27	Toldi Frog									80		80	90
6292/32	Dangling Frog "Cappy"							60	72	110		110	123
6294/32	Dangling Mouse "Pieps"							60	72			110	123
6462/27	Frog (Hand Puppet)	26	28									50	56
6470/27	Owl (Hand Puppet)	30	33									55	62
6472/27	Fox (Hand Puppet)	33	36									62	69
6496/32	Happy Hedgehog										95	95	106
6497/32	Happy Fox										115	115	129
6995/30	Owl (Hand Puppet)	50	55									85	95
7170/06	Guniea Pig	9	9									15	17
7173/06	Hampster	8	8									12	13
7180/05	Frog	7	8	8	8							14	16
7180/07	Frog	8	10	10	10							16	18
7354/04	Mouse, White	5	7	7	7							9	10
7355/04	Mouse, Grey	5	7	7	7							9	10
7370/03	Lady Bug	5	6	7								9	10
7370/04	Lady Bug	4	5	5	6							7	8
7370/06	Lady Bug	5	7	7	8							9	10
7480/06	Owl	7	9	9	9							12	13
7480/09	Owl	9	11	11	11							16	18
7493/05	Pitty Fox	6	7									9	10
7502/05	Pitty Squirrel	6	7									9	10
7503/05	Pitty Mice	8	9									14	16
7860/20	Bambi Fawn					34	34	36				75	84
8190/30	Riding Animal, Ladybug/Wheels		185	190	195	195	195	205	250	375		350	392

CHARACTERS

Steiff #	Description	1980-1981	1981-1982	1982-1983	1983-1984	1984-1985	1985-1986	1986	1987	1988	1989	1990	Current
0116/28	Roly Poly Clown w/Rattle 1909, mhr, LE									260	260	260	351
1523/20	Shepherd and His Flock	69	80									320	358
7627/12	Boy Mecki Character	13	16	17	18	20	20	21	27	45	45	45	50
7627/17	Man Mecki Character	32	39	39	41	50	50	53	65	95	95	95	106
7627/28	Man Mecki Character	410	60	61	65	70	70	75	90	145	145	145	162
7627/50	Mecki, Man			180	195	195	195					340	381
7628/12	Girl Mecki Character	13	16	17	18	20	20	21	27	45	45	45	50
7628/17	Woman Mecki Character	32	39	39	41	50	50	53	65	95	95	95	106
7628/28	Woman Mecki Character	410	60	61	65	70	70	75	90	145	145	145	162
7628/50	Mecki, Woman			180	195	195	195					340	381
7635/19	Santa Claus, LE 2000-1985						75	75	75			125	140
7635/28	Santa Claus, LE 1200-1984/2000-1985					95	95	100	100			155	174
7851/25	Doll, Madi			36								65	73
7871/28	Doll, Marion			43	43							80	90
7872/28	Doll, Marc			43	43							80	90
7873/28	Doll, Tanja			43	43							80	90
7874/28	Doll, Michael			43								80	90
7875/28	Doll, Yvonne			43								80	90
7892/40	Doll, Punch			56								100	112

Roly poly clown with Rattle, 0116/28, 1909 Replica, LE,
1988-1990, $351. *Sheila Perry Collection.*

Key: W = World Wide
U = USA
E = England
G = Germany
WDW = Walt Disney World
DL = Disneyland
N/P = No prices available

ANIMALS OF THE WILD

Steiff #	Description	1980-1981	1981-1982	1982-1983	1983-1984	1984-1985	1985-1986	1986	1987	1988	1989	1990	Current
0020/11	Chimp, mhr	9	10	13	15	19	19	20	25	30	30	30	55
0020/13	Chimp, Mini Mohair										50	50	74
0020/16	Chimp, mhr	15	18									90	104
0020/25	Chimp	27	33									68	78
0020/35	Chimp	42	50									90	104
0020/50	Chimp	90	110									180	207
0020/60	Chimp	115	138									235	270
0021/17	Chimp, Mini Mohair										80	80	107
0022/16	Chimp			19								35	40
0022/26	Chimp			37	39	39	39	41	50	80	80	51	59
0022/36	Chimp			54	57	57	57	60	73	115	115	75	86
0022/52	Chimp			115	115	115	115	125	150	215		130	150
0025/23	Mungo, Brown	57	64	65								110	127
0026/23	Mungo, Yellow	57	64	65	65							110	127
0030/35	Orang, Baby	75	85									135	155
0035/35	Gorilla, Baby	75	85									135	155
0040/28	Gibbon, Baby	40	45	46	46	46	46	49	60	85	85	85	98
0040/45	Young Gibbon	64	72									165	190
0040/60	Dangling Beige	116	140	145	145	145	145	155	185			240	276
0045/50	Monkey, Dressed	119	130	135	135							260	299
0079/03	Tree Pavian, Baby	57	64									110	123
0079/05	Tree Pavian, Stand St 24"	360	360	360								595	666
0080/08	Felt Elephant, 1880, 2 yr LE					60	60	60	60	60	60	75	101
0105/17	Penguin with Leather Wings, LE 8000						70	75	75	80	80	155	209
0111/21	Lying Lion, mhr, LE 2000					79	80	85				167	225
0111/35	Lying Lion, mhr, LE 1000					120	125	135	135			265	358
0112/17	Tiger, Lying, mhr, LE 2000				65	68	68	68	68			142	189
0112/28	Tiger, Lying, mhr, LE 2000				90	95	95	95				200	243
0117/18	Brown Reindeer, mhr, LE 4000											100	135
0123/19	Lion w/Tuba, LE									125	125	135	200
0125/24	Jumbo Elephant, Mechanical, mhr, LE									300	300	300	405
0143/19	Chimp w/Unicycle, cover w/mhr, LE										125	125	169
0333/33	Molly Elephant, Sitting									185	185	185	207
0344/99	S Molly Elephant					600	600	650				900	1008
0345/50	Molly Lynx	140	175									230	258
0368/45	Molly Baby Lion										195	125	140
0370/30	Molly Leo Lion							70	85	125	135	87	97
0370/70	Molly Leo Lion								295	400	400	250	280
0371/30	Molly Baby Lion											110	123
0375/45	Lion		175	180	180	180	180	195				342	383
0376/45	Molly Young Tiger										195	125	140
0376/60	Molly Young Tiger										330	330	370
0378/60	Molly Tiger									230	230	230	258
0380/30	Molly Tiger Taky							70	85	125	135	87	97
0381/25	Bagheera Panther	48	53	53								225	252
0381/50	Super Molly Lion, Standing								280	380	380	380	426
0382/22	Baby Hathi Elephant	43	48									225	252
0382/60	Super Molly Lion, Lying								260	360	360	360	403
0383/22	King Louis Chimp	48	53	53								225	252
0385/75	Molly Puma					130	130			250		250	280
0385/98	Molly Puma						295					445	498
0387/75	Molly Panther					130	130	140	170	250	250	250	280
0387/98	Molly Panther						295	310				445	498

(*Left*) Donkey, 0126/20, mechanical, 1909 Replica, LE, 1988-1990, $250.
(*Right*) Jumbo elephant, 0125/24, mechanical, 1988-1990, $405.

Super Molly, 0382/60,
Lion Laying, $403.
Standing Lion,
0381/50, $426.
*Sheila Perry
Collection.*

Molly Jung Tiger, 0376/45, $140. Leopard, 1953 Replica.
Sheila Perry Collection.

Jocko, 0021/17, yellow tag,
$107. Bonbo, 061257, yel-
low tag. *Sheila Perry
Collection.*

Leo, 402463, 1956 Replica, LE 4000, 1992.
Sheila Perry Collection.

ANIMALS OF THE WILD

Steiff #	Description	1980-1981	1981-1982	1982-1983	1983-1984	1984-1985	1985-1986	1986	1987	1988	1989	1990	Current
0390/40	Molly Leopard									160	160	105	118
0390/50	Molly Leopard								175	235	235	235	263
0405/40	Molly Camel									230	230	125	140
0405/60	Molly Camel									315	315	315	353
0411/40	Molly Zebra									125	125	125	140
0420/40	Molly Moose									230		145	162
0500/30	Bamboo Monkey, Light Brown							80	110			110	123
0500/45	Bamboo Monkey, Light Brown								110	150		150	168
0500/55	Bamboo Monkey, Light Brown								175	240		240	269
0505/18	Elephant	38	42	43	43							75	84
0505/30	Bamboo Monkey, Cream							80	110			110	123
0505/45	Bamboo Monkey, Cream								110	150		150	168
0505/55	Bamboo Monkey, Cream								175	240		240	269
0520/50	Bongo Orang., Rust								185	250	250	250	280
0525/50	Bongo Orang., Cream								185	250	250	250	280
0535/32	Baby Gorilla											81	91
0540/45	Gora Gorilla								185	250	250	150	168
0540/60	Gora Gorilla								250	330	330	185	207
0544/99	Gora Gorilla									1800	2000		2240
0595/35	Mammouth, Trampy											105	118
0609/16	Camel, Standing St 63"	2385	2495	2700	2778	2778			3334	4315		3895	4362
0710/35	Kangaroo/Baby	45	50	53	57	57	57	60				85	95
0755/28	Giraffe	30	39	39	39	45	45	48				60	67
0755/40	Giraffe	42	50	51	52	56	56	59				80	90
0755/60	Giraffe	70	89	90	90	90	90					135	151
0759/15	Giraffe St 60", mhr	1377	1450	1557	1557	1557	1557		1945		2593	2350	2632
0759/24	Giraffe St 96", mhr	2340	2500	2655	2655	2655	2655		3334		4769	4350	4872
0800/20	Lion	38	42									75	84
0805/18	Lion, Standing	28										54	60
0805/26	Lion, Standing	39	48									75	84
0805/99	Lion, Standing										5694	6000	6900
0807/99	Lioness, Lying										3750	4000	4750
0809/11	Lion, Standing St 42"	2223	2547	2547	2547	2547	2547		2621			4300	4816
0812/16	Rango Lion	38	43	43	43							75	84
0815/15	Sulla Lioness	35	39	40								70	78
0820/16	Wittie Tiger	35	39	40	40							70	78
0822/99	Tiger, Standing St 59"	1800	2000	2210	2210	2210	2210		2778			3975	4200
0825/16	Sigi Leopard	35	39	40	40							70	78
0870/60	Tiger Cub Pascha					155	155	165	200	265	265	265	297
0885/50	Leopard, Lying			105	105	105	105					195	218
0890/40	Leopard Cub	140	160	165	165							295	330
0892/40	Kango Kangaroo with Baby										210	140	157
1150/45	Seal Robby											96	108
1170/16	Walrus									65	65	42	47
1172/80	Walrus									375	375	375	420
1172/99	Walrus									1600	1600	1600	1792
1174/55	Walrus									215		215	255
1175/14	Seal	31	35	36	36	36	36					60	67
1175/20	Seal	49	59	60								95	106
1178/14	Seal	31	38	38	38	38	38					60	67
1179/04	Sealion Cub	125	140	145								235	263
1305/09	Jumbo Elephant, Mini-Mohair										50	50	55
1305/12	Jumbo Elephant, Mini-Mohair										70	70	78
1448/13	Kango Kangaroo										50	50	56
1450/12	Jumbo Elephant	17	20	21	23	29						39	45
1451/09	Rhino	16	18	19	19							39	44
1451/12	Jumbo Elephant						23	24	30	50	50	32	36
1453/14	Hockey Dromedary	17	20	21	23							39	44

Key: W = World Wide • U = USA • E = England • G = Germany • WDW = Walt Disney World • DL = Disneyland • N/P = No prices available

ANIMALS OF THE WILD

Steiff #	Description	1980-1981	1981-1982	1982-1983	1983-1984	1984-1985	1985-1986	1986	1987	1988	1989	1990	Current
1453/15	Trampy Camel						23	24	30	50		50	56
1456/09	Nosy Rhino						23	24	30	50		50	56
1457/14	Elk	25	28	28								60	67
1458/12	Bison	22	24	25								50	56
1460/13	Lion	17	20	21	23	31						39	44
1461/12	Leo Lion						23	24	30	50	50	32	36
1463/18	Gaty Crocodile						27	29	35	55	55	55	62
1468/10	Wild Boar	19	21	21	21	21	21	22	27	40		39	44
1472/07	Dolphin	11	14	14	14	14	14	15	18	30	30	30	34
1473/09	Seal	13	16	17	18	18	18	19	23	40	40	40	45
1474/10	Walrus	16	17	18	18	18						39	44
1512/16	Ossi, Zebra			25	26	26	26					48	54
2040/25	Putsi Otter, Standing								85	110		115	129
2045/25	Putsi Otter, Sitting								85	110		115	129
2160/20	Otty Otter			30								55	62
2251/18	Guinea Pig Ginny											37	41
2251/22	Guinea Pig Ginny											44	49
2270/25	Otter	32	32									65	73
2270/35	Otter	54										95	106
2300/10	Fish, Blue, mhr	8	9									40	45
2301/10	Fish, Gold, mhr	8	9									40	45
2311/25	Fish, Green	28										52	58
2320/25	Dolphin	23	26	27	27							44	49
2320/35	Dolphin	28	33	33	33							55	62
2322/35	Finny Dolphin								57	75		75	84
2322/50	Finny Dolphin								89	120		120	134
2322/99	Finny Dolphin								450	600		600	672
2505/12	Penguin	16	19	19	20	20	20	21	26	37	37	37	41
2505/27	Penguin	35	40	41								70	78
2505/40	Penguin	59	77									115	129
2507/20	Baby Penguin				33	33	33	35	42	70	70	70	78
2507/38	Penguin			72	72	72	72	76	92	135		130	146
2509/09	Penguin St 36"	450	450	450	450	450	450		620		834	850	952
2510/40	Charly Penguin								115	150	150	150	168
2511/26	Paddy Puffin	57	65									115	129
2531/13	Parakeet, Gold/Green	18	22	23	23	23	23					54	60
2534/13	Parakeet, White/Blue	18	22	23	23	23	23	25	30	47	47	47	53
2540/30	Parrot, Red, Studio	76	89	90	90	90	90		130			225	252
2541/30	Parrot, Blue, Studio	76	89	90	90	90	90		130			225	252
2544/30	Lora Parrot, Red								95	125		125	140
2545/30	Cockatoo			90	90	90						180	202
2550/30	Lora Parrot, Green								95	125		165	185
2555/14	Parrot Lori											45	50
2560/14	Tucan Tucky											45	50
2560/20	Tucky Tucan										105	105	118
2565/14	Pelican Peli											45	50
2565/20	Peli Pelican										105	105	118
2570/14	Penguin Peggy											45	50
2605/20	Kingfisher 8"	82	82									158	177
2606/50	Heron 20"	190	190	195	195	195						360	403
2608/50	Stork 20"	200	200	200	200	200						380	426
2612/20	Swan, White				40	40	40					75	84
2615/28	Falcon, Studio	85	97	99	99	99	99	105	125	195		200	224
2620/99	Peacock, Studio	800	950	1000	1000	1000	1000		1400	1600	1963	1700	1904
2621/80	Peacock, Studio	750	900	900	1000							1500	1680
2650/23	Young Wild Boar									120		120	134
2655/28	Young Wild Boar Wutzi											100	111

(Left) Chimp, Mini, 0021/17, 1989-1990, $107.
(Middle) Chimp, Mini, 0020/13, 1989-1990, $74.
(Right) Chimp, 0022/26, 1982-1990, $59.

Maxi, 032806; Fiep, 1308/12, $67; Peggy, 1957 Replica, 033018; Joggi, 032288. All mohair. *Sheila Perry Collection.*

Previous Page: Jumbo Elephant, Mechanical, 0125/24, LE, 1988-1990, $405.

Steiff #	Description	1980-1981	1981-1982	1982-1983	1983-1984	1984-1985	1985-1986	1986	1987	1988	1989	1990	Current
2655/40	Young Wild Boar Wutzi											135	151
2660/20	Bora Wild Boar								57	75		75	84
2660/30	Bora Wild Boar								89	120		120	134
2675/15	Wild Boar	33	39	39	39	39	39					65	73
2675/20	Wild Boar			50	52	65	65					90	101
2677/30	Baby Boar			81	81	81	81	86				140	157
2678/50	Wild Boar St		230	235	235	235						425	476
2690/32	Scottish Highland Bull									180	180	180	202
2695/35	Buffalo									200	200	200	224
2897/30	Jr. Leo Lion Cub			91	95	95	95	100	100	180	180	180	202
2912/18	Snuffy Elephant								50	65		65	73
2914/18	Snuffy Lion								55	75	75	75	84
3247/26	Swan	57	65	66								140	157
3475/40	Elbow Puppet-Leopard	74	80	82								140	157
3478/50	Elbow Puppet-Puma/Lion	86	94									170	190
3518/14	Snuffy Lion	19	24	24								38	43
3518/18	Snuffy Lion	25	32	32								50	56
5322/35	Panther, Lying	58	75									110	123
5322/50	Panther, Lying	98										180	202
5340/33	Cosy Elephant, Lying									120		120	134
5350/15	Cosy Jumbo Elephant					39	39	41	52	70	70	70	78
5350/22	Cosy Jumbo Elephant					60	60	64	80	110		110	123
5350/30	Cosy Jumbo Elephant					100	100					165	185
5351/40	Leopard, Lying	76	84	85								140	157
5352/25	Cosy Elephant			58	58							95	106
5370/28	Cosy Panther	57	63	63	63	63	63	67	82	110		110	123
5372/33	Cosy Puma		64	65	65	65	65					120	134
5374/17	Cosy Seal					25	25	27	33	45		45	50
5374/35	Cosy Seal			49	49	49	49	52	63	90		90	101
5375/30	Cosy Seal Robby, Grey							45	58	85		85	95
5375/31	Cosy Seal Robby, Beige							45	58	85		85	95
5375/57	Cosy Seal			81	81	81	81					145	162
5376/50	Cosy Seal		125	126								230	258
5387/27	Cosy Whale				27	27	27	29	36	55		45	50
5410/80	Cosy Dolphin		157									250	280
5420/19	Cosy Nosy Rhino, Lying									95		95	106
5420/75	Cosy Nosy Rhino, Lying									300		300	336
5420/99	Cosy Nosy Rhino, Lying									1600		1600	1792
5422/20	Cosy Nosy Rhino, Standing									95		95	106
5422/40	Cosy Nosy Rhino, Standing									150		150	168
5438/25	Dolphin Finny, Ice Blue									53		53	59
5450/27	Cosy Gora Monkey		79	80	80							145	162
5578/11	Penquin								23	30		32	36
5585/15	Blue Dolphin								23	35		35	39
5588/15	Grey Dolphin								23	35		35	39
5655/16	Mini Floppy Elephant										53	53	59
5706/20	Kiddi Elephant										75	75	84
5710/20	Elephant	45										80	90
5710/30	Elephant	61	66									110	123
5715/20	Cocki	41	44	45								75	84
5715/30	Cocki	59	65									110	123
5810/22	Elephant	43	48	49	49	49						79	88
6190/30	Chimp	38	47									75	84
6215/28	Possy Guenon Monkey										120	120	134
6220/28	Possy Elephant										125	125	137
6228/28	Possy Lion										120	120	134
6240/20	Toldi Chimp			25	28							46	52
6240/30	Toldi Chimp			49	53							90	101

ANIMALS OF THE WILD

Steiff #	Description	1980-1981	1981-1982	1982-1983	1983-1984	1984-1985	1985-1986	1986	1987	1988	1989	1990	Current
6271/27	Toldi Elephant									85		85	95
6272/27	Toldi Monkey									80		80	90
6280/70	Dangling Monkey											240	269
6285/55	Lulac Tiger			125	125	125	125					235	263
6288/32	Dangling Monkey Mungo							60	72			110	123
6304/50	Hippo	170										300	336
6305/50	Rhino	170										300	336
6310/60	Bison	175	195	200	200	200						325	364
6314/60	Tiger	138	150	155	155							270	302
6315/30	Puma, Lying	75	75									145	162
6315/40	Puma, Standing	80	87									155	174
6315/99	Puma, Lying	375		425	425	425						750	840
6316/99	Puma, Sitting	590		700	700	700						1100	1232
6320/30	Leopard, Lying	75	82									145	162
6320/40	Leopard, Standing	80	80									155	174
6320/99	Leopard, Lying	375	415	425	425	425	425					750	840
6321/99	Leopard, Standing	590	650	675	675	675	675					1100	1499
6322/99	Leopard, Sitting St	695	713	700	700	700	700					1300	1456
6323/99	Panther, Lying	375	415	425	425	425						750	840
6325/99	Panther, Standing	590	650	675	675	675						1100	1232
6460/27	Chimpanzee (Hand Puppet)	26	28	28	28	28	28	30	36			50	56
6471/27	Lion (Hand Puppet)	33	36	37	37	37	37	39	47			62	69
6474/27	Wolf (Hand Puppet)	33	36									62	69
6476/27	Crocodile (Hand Puppet)	33	36									62	69
6488/32	Happy Guenon Monkey										105	105	118
6820/18	Lion (Hand Puppet), mhr	23										90	101
6880/17	Tiger (Hand Puppet), mhr	23										90	101
6991/30	Chimpanzee (Hand Puppet)	46	50	51	51	51	51	54	65			85	110
7086/10	Wool Bird Assmt	10	10									16	18
7116/08	Birds, Assmt	5	7	7	7							11	12
7276/09	Fish, Assmt	10	11									19	21
7390/10	Penquin	8	10									15	17
7500/05	Pitty Elephant	6	7									9	10
7501/05	Pitty Lion	6	7									9	10

Key: W = World Wide • U = USA • E = England • G = Germany • WDW = Walt Disney World • DL = Disneyland • N/P = No prices available

Steiff #	Description	1980-1981	1981-1982	1982-1983	1983-1984	1984-1985	1985-1986	1986	1987	1988	1989	1990	Current
4003	Goldilocks 16" & 3 Steiff Bears, Reeves International, (0173/25, Boy; 0173/30, Mother; 0173/32, Father), 1984, Offered at $200 U												750
4004	Goldilocks 8" & 3 Steiff Bears, Reeves International, 0173/25. Boy; 0173/18, Mother; 0173/22 Father), 1985, Offered at $200 U												450
4005	Alice & Her Friends, (13cm Steiff Cat; 13cm Steiff Mouse; 20cm Steiff Rabbit w/big pocket watch), LE 3000, 1986, Offered at $250 U												400
51847	Petsil, The Toy Store, LE, 1500, 1993 U												175
00206	Teddy Donald, 99cm WDW, LE 2, 1993 U												N/P
120/19	Bear Band Leader w/Baton, LE									125	125	135	195
0020/11	Chimp, mhr	9	10	13	15	19	19	20	25	30	30	30	55
0020/13	Chimp, Mini Mohair										50	50	74
0020/16	Chimp, mhr	15	18								90		104
0020/25	Chimp	27	33									68	78
0020/35	Chimp	42	50									90	104
0020/50	Chimp	90	110									180	207
0020/60	Chimp	115	138									235	270
0021/17	Chimp, Mini Mohair										80	80	107
0022/16	Chimp			19								35	40
0022/26	Chimp			37	39	39	39	41	50	80	80	51	59
0022/36	Chimp			54	57	57	57	60	73	115	115	75	86
0022/52	Chimp			115	115	115	115	125	150	215		130	150
0025/23	Mungo, Brown	57	64	65								110	127
0026/23	Mungo, Yellow	57	64	65	65							110	127
0030/35	Orang, Baby	75	85									135	155
0035/35	Gorilla, Baby	75	85									135	155
0040/28	Gibbon, Baby	40	45	46	46	46	46	49	60	85	85	85	98
0040/45	Young Gibbon	64	72									165	190
0040/60	Dangling Beige	116	140	145	145	145	145	155	185			240	276
0045/50	Monkey, Dressed	119	130	135	135							260	299
0050/28	Dinosaur, 1959, LE 4000											200	270
0055/00	Eric Bat Set, 2 pc., 1960, LE 4000											200	270
0079/03	Tree Pavian, Baby	57	64									110	123
0079/05	Tree Pavian, Stand St 24"	360	360	360								595	666
0080/08	Felt Elephant, 1880, 2 yr LE					60	60	60	60	60	60	75	101
0081/14	Felt Duck, 1892 Rep., LE 4000									125	125	125	169
0082/20	Roly Poly Bear, 1894, 2 yr LE					69	70	70	70	80	80	95	150
0085/12	Bear on Wheels, LE 12,000						95	100	100	120	120	165	175
0090/11	Polar Bear Jntd Legs/Rtng Head, LE 3000								95	95		155	200
0091/14	Pig, Univ Head Movement, 1909, LE 4000										155	155	225
0093/12	Fox, 1910, LE 4000									150	150		203
0095/17	Begging Rabbit 7x Jntd 1911, LE 4000									145	145	145	196
0100/86	Elephant on Wheels w/Circus Calp., LE							2100	2100	2100		1200	1200
0100/87	Circus Cage w/Lying Lion, LE									275		550	325
0100/88	Circus Wagon w/Giraffe, LE										325	450	350
0100/89	Circus Wagon w/Tiger, LE										350	550	375
0100/90	Circus Wagon w/Two Bears, LE											450	475
0101/14	Bully Dog, 1927 Rep., LE 6000							75	75	120		145	225
0104/10	Tabby Cat, 1928 Rep., LE 6000							75	75	120		130	176
0105/17	Penguin with Leather Wings, LE 8000						70	75	75	80	80	155	209
0108/14	Drinking Cat, 1933, LE 4000											185	250
0111/21	Lying Lion, mhr, LE 2000					79	80	85				167	225
0111/35	Lying Lion, mhr, LE 1000					120	125	135	135			265	358
0112/17	Tiger, Lying, mhr, LE 2000				65	68	68	68	68			142	189
0112/28	Tiger, Lying, mhr, LE 2000				90	95	95	95				200	243
011382	Teddys Teddy Baby, 19cm, Teddys, LE 1000, 1991 U												295
0115/18	Roly Poly Bear w/Rattle 1908, mhr, LE									125	125	125	145
0116/25	Record Teddy, 1913, LE 4000, 1990 W											300	350
0116/28	Roly Poly Clown w/Rattle 1909, mhr, LE									260	260	260	351
0117/18	Brown Reindeer, mhr, LE 4000											100	135
0118/00	Sleigh Set, mhr, LE 6000, 1989 U										275	275	350
0118/25	Boxer, Lying, mhr, LE 2000					55	57	57	57	57			85
011863	Minnie Bear, WDW, LE 1500, 1992 U												650
011863	Minnie Bear, 80cm, WDW, LE 1, 1992 U												N/P
011863	Minnie Bear, 99cm, WDW, LE 1, 1992 U												N/P

Key: W = World Wide • U = USA • E = England • G = Germany • WDW = Walt Disney World • DL = Disneyland • N/P = No prices available

Numerical Listing

Steiff #	Description	1980-1981	1981-1982	1982-1983	1983-1984	1984-1985	1985-1986	1986	1987	1988	1989	1990	Current
011870	Minnie Bear, 60cm, WDW, LE 20, 1992 U												2200
011894	Harrods Musical Bear 1926, LE 2000, 1992 E												N/P
011979	Teddile, The Toy Store, LE 1000, 1992 U												275
011986	Antique Teddy, Grey, 30cm, DL, LE 1500, 1992 U												300
011993	Antique Teddy, Grey, 60cm, DL, LE 20, 1992 U												1500
012006	Antique Teddy, Grey, 80cm, DL, LE 1, 1992 U												N/P
012013	Antique Teddy, Grey, 99cm, DL, LE 1, 1992 U												N/P
0120/19	Bear Band Leader w/ Baton, LE									125	125	135	195
0120/19	Bear Band Leader, LE, 5000, 1988 U												185
0121/19	Dog w/Trombone, LE									125	125	135	200
0122/19	Cat W/Drum, LE									125	125	135	200
0123/19	Lion w/Tuba, LE									125	125	135	200
0124/19	Crocodile w/Trumpet, LE									125	125	135	200
0125/24	Jumbo Elephant, Mechanical, mhr, LE									300	300	300	405
0126/20	Donkey Mechanical 1909 Rep, LE									185	185	185	250
0128/33	Bear w/Snow White & Rose Red Set, Suzanne Gibson Doll Reeves International, 1987, LE 2000 U												400
0130/17	Unicorn, Lying, LE 2000				40	42						135	160
0130/27	Unicorn, Lying, LE 2000				55	57						175	195
0130/28	Bear on 4 Legs, Univ. Head Mov., mhr, LE 4000										400	400	550
0131/00	Rub-A-Dub-Dub Set 3 Bears in a Tub 1988, LE 2000 U								275	275		310	350
0131/23	Rub-A-Dub-Dub Set, yellow, Baker, LE 2000 U												140
0131/24	Rub-A-Dub-Dub Set, brass, Candlemaker, LE 2000, 1988 U												140
0131/25	Rub-A-Dub-Dub Set, brown butcher, LE 2000, 1988 U												140
0132/24	Wigwag Seesaw P-Toy w/Two Bears, mhr, LE 4000, 1988 U									260	260	260	260
0134/22	Niki Rabbit, mhr					58						155	209
0134/28	Niki Rabbit, mhr					70	75					195	263
0135/00	Hoppy Rabbit Set, 3 Pieces, 1984 U				265								358
0135/20	Baby Bear Pull Toy with wagon, 1908 Rep, cover w/mhr, LE 4000 W										275	275	300
0140/38	Klein Archie, Enchanted Dollhouse, LE 2500 U												175
0143/19	Chimp w/Unicycle, cover w/mhr, LE										125	125	169
0144/19	Gorilla Strong Man, mhr, LE 5000											125	169
0145/12	Lamb							30	30			30	41
0145/19	Elephant Balloon Seller, mhr, LE										135	135	182
0146/13	Cat, Crouching							50	50	50		50	68
0146/19	Hippo Fat Lady, mhr, LE										135	135	182
0147/12	Seal w/Ball, Stand, mhr, LE										100	100	145
0147/20	Rabbit, Begging							50	50			50	68
0148/03	Teddy Bear Pin				9							15	35
0149/19	Fire Eater Dragon, mhr, LE 5000											125	150
0150/32	Richard Steiff 1902-1903 Bear, LE 20,000 W				90	100						285	400
0151/25	Mr. Cinnamon Bear, (1904), LE, 1984 U					70	75	79				165	275
0151/26	Mr. Cinnamon Bear, 1984												275
0151/27	Harrods Musical Bear 1904/05, LE 2000, 1990 E												395
0151/32	Mr. Cinnamon Bear, (1904), LE, 1984 U					85	90	95				265	350
0151/40	Mr. Cinnamon Bear, (1904), LE, 1984 U					125	135	145				435	450
0151/55	Mr. Cinnamon Bear (1904), LE 1985 U												500
0152/25	Mr. Vanilla, Hobby Center Toys, LE 1000, 1989 U												475
0153/43	Papa Bar, 100th Annv, LE 5,000, Original Teddy U	150										800	1000
0155/00	Hoppy Rabbit Set, 3pc. 1984, LE					150	150	150				265	358
0155/15	Christening Bear, 1986, LE U							60	75	75		99	150
0155/18	Roly Poly Bear with rattle, 1908 Rep, 1990 U												150
0155/22	Santa's Elf, LE									100	100	125	225
0155/22	Flower Bear-er, L.E. 2000 pc, 1985 U						75	80	100	100		125	175
0155/23	Ring Bear-er, L.E. 2000 pc. 1985 U						75	80	100	100		125	175
0155/26	Margaret Strong Bear, mhr, LE, 1984 U			48	48	50	53	56	69	100	100	100	120
0155/32	Margaret Strong Bear, mhr, LE, 1984 U			62	62	65	69	73	89	135	135	135	160
0155/34	Victorian Girl Bear 1986, LE 1200 U							125				225	250
0155/35	Victorian Boy Bear 1986, LE 1200 U							125	125			225	250
0155/36	Bride, L.E. 2000, 1984 U					100	110	125	150	200	200	215	300
0155/37	Groom, L.E. 2000, 1984 U					100	110	125	150	200	200	215	300
0155/38	Mama & Baby, L.E. 8,000, mhr, 7500 U		150									495	600

NUMERICAL LISTING

Steiff #	Description	1980-1981	1981-1982	1982-1983	1983-1984	1984-1985	1985-1986	1986	1987	1988	1989	1990	Current
0155/38	Santa Bear, 1000 pc, 1986 U							125	150	200	200	200	300
0155/42	Margaret Strong Bear, mhr, LE, 1983 U				90	95	100	105	125	200	200	200	240
0155/51	Margaret Strong Gold Bear, mhr, LE, 1983 U					185	195	205	250	350	350	350	360
0155/60	Margaret Strong Gold Bear, mhr, LE, 1984 U					250	285	300	375	495	495	495	425
0156/00	Margaret Strong Cinnamon Bear Set, mhr, LE 2,000, 1984 U					300	300					590	900
0156/26	Cinnamon Bear, mhr, LE							53				100	250
0156/32	Cinnamon Bear, mhr							69				135	350
0156/34	Captain Strong Bear, 1987, LE U									200	200	215	275
0156/36	M. Strong Victorian Lady, LE, 1987 U								150	150	150	195	250
0156/37	M. Strong Victorian Gentleman, LE, 1987 U								150	150	150	195	250
0156/38	St. Nicholas Bear, Vic. Santa Bxd, 1200 pc, 1987								150	200	200	200	300
0156/42	Cinnamon Bear, mhr, LE							100				195	450
0157/26	Margaret Strong Cream Bear, mhr, LE, 1984 U					50	53	56				145	250
0157/32	Margaret Strong Cream Bear, mhr, LE, 1984 U					65	69	73				185	350
0157/42	Margaret Strong Cream Bear, mhr, LE, 1984 U					95	100	105				265	450
0157/51	Margaret Strong Cream Bear, mhr, LE, 1985 U						195	205				565	700
0157/60	Margaret Strong Cream Bear, mhr, LE, 1985 U						285	300				625	1200
0158/17	Druckknopfbar, (Push Button Bear), 1908 Rep, LE 50,000, 1989 W												N/P
0158/17	Snap-Apart Bear, mhr, LE 5000										135	275	300
0158/25	Margaret Strong White Bear, Leather Paws, mhr, LE 3000 U						60	60	60			165	400
0158/31	Margaret Strong White Bear, Leather Paws, mhr, LE 2500 U						79	79	79			255	600
0158/41	Margaret Strong White Bear, Leather Paws, mhr, LE 2000 U							110	110	110		325	1000
0158/50	Margaret Strong White Bear, Leather Paws, mhr, 750 U							225				1200	1600
0159/26	Antique Teddy Schwarz, J.P. Bear, Mary D's Dolls & Bears & Such, LE 1000, 1990 U												275
0160/00	M. Strong Choc. Brown Set, 4pc. LE 2000 U				275							480	850
0162/00	Giengen Teddy Set, "The Birthplace of the Teddy," LE 1600, 1984 W					150	159	159	159			260	375
0162/33	Teddy Bear 1906, FAO 125th Year Anniversary, LE 1,000, 1987 U												450
0163/19	Teddy Clown Junior, White Tag, LE U								50			195	225
0163/19	Teddy Clown Junior, Yellow Tag, LE 5000, 1987 U								50			125	175
0163/20	Clown Teddy, mhr, LE 5000									100	100		175
0163/26	Hamleys Bear, LE 2000, 1988 E												350
0163/34	White Teddy Bear, 1909, FAO Schwarz, LE 2000, 1988 U												350
	Maulkorb- Teddy Bear, 1908, LE 5000, 1991 U												N/P
0164/29	Somersault Bear, 1909 Rep, mhr, LE 5000, 1990 W											395	475
0164/30	Circus Dolly Bear (Rare Pale Yellow) 1987 approx. 800 Pieces								135			245	375
0164/31	Circus Dolly Bear/Yellow, mhr, LE 2000, white tag, 1987 U								135	175	175	185	250
0164/32	Circus Dolly Bear/Green, mhr, LE 2000, white tag, 1987 U								135	175	175	185	250
0164/34	Circus Dolly Bear/Violet, mhr, LE 2000, white tag, 1987 U								135	175	175	185	250
0165/28	1909 Gold Teddy, mhr, 1983 W					55	59	62	62			75	270
0165/38	1909 Gold Teddy Bear, mhr, 1983 W				80	85	90	95				110	358
0165/51	1909 Gold Teddy, mhr, 1983 W					150	159	169				435	587
0165/60	1909 Gold Teddy, mhr, 1984 W						275	290	290			580	945
0166/25	Blond Teddy, 1909, mhr, 1988 W									100	100	100	134
0166/29	W. Shakespeare Bear, 1909 Rep, LE 2000, 1987 E												N/P
0166/32	Preppy Bear 35 (blue shirt, pants & sweater), Polo, Ralph Lauren, NY, 1991/92 U												350
0166/35	Blond Teddy, 1909, mhr, 1988 W									145	145	145	196
0166/43	Blond Teddy, 1909, mhr, 1988 W									225	225	225	304
0167/22	Giengen Bear, Grey, 1906 Rep, mhr, 1986 U							55	69	100	100	100	150
0167/23	Teddy Schwarz, 40th Birthday UFDC, LE 360, 1989 U												N/P
0167/26	Giengen Teddy Bear Grey, 1906 Rep, 1985 U												185
0167/32	Giengen Bear, Grey, 1906 Rep, mhr, 1985 U						85	90	100	160	160	160	225

Key: W = World Wide • U = USA • E = England • G = Germany • WDW = Walt Disney World • DL = Disneyland • N/P = No prices available

Steiff #	Description	1980-1981	1981-1982	1982-1983	1983-1984	1984-1985	1985-1986	1986	1987	1988	1989	1990	Current
0167/42	Giengen Bear, Grey, 1906 Rep, mhr, 1985 U						120	125	150	225	225	225	350
0167/52	Giengen Bear, Grey, 1906 Rep, mhr, 1986 U							195	250	350	350	350	140
0168/22	Giengen Bear, Blond, 1906 Rep, mhr, 1986 U							55	69	100	100	100	140
0168/28	Hamleys Bear, LE 2000, 1989 E												250
0168/32	Giengen Teddy Bear, Blond, 1988 W												225
0168/42	Giengen Bear, Blond, 1906 Rep, mhr, 1986 U							125	150	225		235	300
0169/40	Happy Anniversary, 1926 Rep, LE 6000, 1991 W												N/P
0169/65	Happy Anniversary, 1926 Rep, LE 5000, 1990 U										525		1100
0170/32	Teddy Clown 1926 Rep, LE 10,000, 1986 W							150	150			395	400
0171/25	Teddy Rose, LE											195	275
0171/41	Teddy Rose w/Ctr. Seam, (1925) LE 10,000, 1987 W								1100	300	230	345	500
0172/17	Dicky Bear, blond (for Circus wagon), LE 5000, 1990 U												130
0172/18	Dicky Bear Rose, The Toy Store, LE 1000, 1991 (set) U												300
0172/19	Dicky Bear Mauve, The Toy Store, LE 1000, 1991 (set) U												300
0172/32	Dicky Bear, 1930 Rep, LE 20,000, 1985 W						100	105	105	125		225	275
0172/32	Dicky "Clowns Around", Ronald McDonald House U												650
0173/14	Goldilock Bear Boy (part of set #4004), LE, 1985 U												150
0173/18	Goldilock Bear Mother (part of set #4004), LE,												200
0173/22	Goldilock Bear Boy (part of set #4004), LE, 1985 U												175
0173/25	Goldilock Bear Father (part of set #4004), LE, 1985 U												200
0173/30	Goldilock Bear Mother (part of set #4003), LE 1984 U												250
0173/32	Goldilocks Bear, Father (part of set #4003), LE, 1984 U												275
0173/33	Teddy Hellbrauh, 1906 Rep, LE 3000, 1989 G												N/P
0173/40	Black Bear, 1907 Rep, LE 4000, 1988 W									300	300	600	800
0174/35	Muzzle Bear, White, 1908 Rep, LE 6000, 1990 W											295	270
0174/46	Muzzle Bear, White, 1908 Rep, mhr, LE 5000, 1989 U									375	375	375	450
0174/60	Muzzle Bear, White, 1908 Rep, mhr, LE 2650, 1989 U									500	500		700
0174/61	Teddy, 1907 Rep, Light Brown, (Moveable Head), LE 2000, 1989 G												N/P
0174/61	British Collectors Bear, LE 2000, 1989 E												800
0175/19	Teddy Baby Ringmaster, mhr, LE 5,000, 1989 U										140	140	200
0175/29	Teddy Baby, 1930 Rep, Brown, mhr, LE, 1984 U					85	95	100	125	175	175	175	275
0175/35	Teddy Baby, 1930 Rep, Brown, mhr, LE, 1984 U					110	125	135	165	225	225	225	350
0175/42	Teddy Baby, 1930 Rep, brown, mhr, LE, 1984 U					165	175	185	235	300	300	300	400
0176/29	Teddy Baby, 1930 Rep, blond, mhr, LE, 1985 U						95	100				245	200
0176/35	Teddy Baby, 1930 Rep, blond, mhr, LE, 1985 U						125	135	135			265	250
0176/42	Teddy Baby, 1930 Rep, blond, mhr, LE, 1985 U						175	185				400	350
0177/00	Teddy Baby & Wolf Set, Zum 85 Jahrigen Jubilaum der Firma Paul Wolff, Grengen, LE 1000, 1988 G												650
0177/19	Teddy Baby Food Vendor, mhr, LE 5000, 1990 U										140		175
0178/29	1938 Panda, mhr, LE					85	85				265		250
0178/35	1938 Panda, mhr, LE					110	110					320	350
0179/19	Teddy Baby Rose, Hobby Center Toys, LE 1000, 1990 U												375
0180/50	Petsy Bi-Color, 1927 Rep, LE 6000, 1981 U												700
0180/50	Petsy Bear, Ctr. Seam Bicolor, mhr, LE 5000, 1989/90 U										375	375	700
0181/35	Petsy Bear, Replica, Ctr Seam Brass, mhr, LE 5000 W										225	225	395
0181/36	Hamleys Bear Oliver, LE 2000, 1990 E												N/P
0184/35	Alfonzo, Teddy Bears of Whitney, LE 5000, 1990 E												500
0188/25	Teddy Bear Replica 1955 mit Halsmechanik, LE 4000, 1990 W												300
0190/17	Jackie Bear, 1953 Rep, mhr, LE 12,000 W										135	135	175
0190/25	Jackie Bear, 1953 Rep, mhr, LE 10,000, 1987 W							110	135		295		275
0190/35	Jackie Bear, 1953 Rep, mhr, LE 4000, 1988 U									300	300	300	350
0201/10	Beige Teddy Bear, Jointed, mhr, LE					35	36					88	100
0201/11	Original Teddy, Beige, mhr	9	10	13	15	19	20	21	25	30	30	30	70
0201/14	Beige Teddy Bear, Jointed, mhr, LE				25	30	30					75	125
	Nicholaus Bar, Hobby Center Toys, LE 300, 1985 U												450
	Frau Nikolaus, Hobby Center Toys, LE 150, 1986 U												400
0201/14	Hans Helfer, Hobby Center Toys, LE 200, 1987 U												250
0201/18	Original Teddy, Beige, mhr				30	35	37	39	47	70	70	70	125

Steiff #	Description	1980-1981	1981-1982	1982-1983	1983-1984	1984-1985	1985-1986	1986	1987	1988	1989	1990	Current
0201/26	Original Teddy, Beige, mhr	27	30	33	36	40	43	45	55	85	85	85	150
0201/36	Original Teddy, Beige, mhr	36	40	48	50	55	59	62	75	115	115	115	225
0201/41	Original Teddy Bear, Beige, mhr			70	75	75	79	85	100	160	160	160	275
0201/51	Original Teddy Bear, Beige, mhr			115	120	120	125	135	165	250	250	250	350
0201/75	Original Teddy Bear, Beige, mhr				450	500	529	560	675	975	975	975	1300
0201/99	Original Bear Beige, mhr			700	700	750	795	850	9100	1450		2300	3000
0202/10	Caramel Teddy Bear, Jointed, mhr, LE					35	36					88	100
0202/11	Original Teddy, Caramel, mhr	9	10	13	15	19	20	21	25	30	30	30	70
0202/12	Original Teddy, Caramel, Mini-Mohair										50	50	70
0202/14	Caramel Teddy Bear, Jointed, mhr, LE U					25	30	30				75	125
0202/15	Original Teddy, Caramel, Mini-Mohair										70	70	100
0202/18	Original Teddy, Caramel, mhr					30	35	37	39	47	70	70	125
0202/26	Original Teddy, Caramel, mhr	27	30	33	36	40	43	45	55	85	85	85	150
0202/36	Original Teddy, Caramel, mhr	36	40	48	50	55	59	62	75	115	115	115	225
0202/41	Original Teddy, Caramel, mhr	53	60	70	75	75	79	85	100	160	160	160	275
0202/51	Original Teddy, Caramel, mhr	84	100	115	120	120	125	135	165	250	250	250	350
0202/75	Original Teddy, Caramel, mhr				450	500	529	560	675	975		1195	1300
0202/99	Original Teddy, Caramel, mhr				700	750	795	850	9100	1450		2300	3105
0203/00	White Orig. Bears w/Paws, 5 pc.											625	844
0203/10	White Teddy Bear, Jointed, mhr, LE					35	36					88	125
0203/11	Original Teddy Bear, White, mhr			13	15	19	20	21	25			39	80
0203/14	White Teddy Bear, Jointed, mhr, LE				25	30	30	30	30			75	135
0203/18	Original Teddy, White, mhr				30	35	37	39	47			87	152
0203/26	Original Teddy Bear, White, mhr			33	36	40	43	45	55			110	192
0203/36	Original Teddy Bear, White, mhr			48	50	55	59	62	75			175	306
0203/41	Original Teddy Bear, White, mhr			70	75	75	79	85	100			235	411
0203/51	Original Teddy Bear, White, mhr				120	120	125	135	165			310	543
0203/75	Original Teddy Bear, White, mhr				450	500						1250	1688
0203/99	Original Teddy Bear, White, mhr				700	750						2800	3780
0204/16	1982 The Teddy Tea Party, LE 10,000 U			175								300	675
0205/26	Original Teddy, Caramel	32	35	37	37	45	45	48	58			80	108
0205/35	Original Teddy, Caramel	45	50	52	54	62	62	66	80			110	149
0205/50	Original Teddy, Caramel	97	105	120	120	120						235	317
0206/10	Chocolate Teddy Bear, Jointed, mhr, LE					35	36					88	119
0206/11	Original Teddy, Choc. Brown, mhr					19	20	21	25	30	30	30	65
0206/14	Chocolate Teddy Bear, Jointed, mhr, LE					30	30	30				75	125
0206/18	Original Teddy, Chocolate Brown, mhr					35	37	39	47	70	70	70	123
0206/26	Original Teddy, Chocolate Brown, mhr					40	43	45	55	85	85	85	149
0206/36	Original Teddy, Chocolate Brown, mhr					55	59	62	75	115	115	115	201
0206/41	Original Teddy, Chocolate Brown, mhr					75	79	85	100	160	160	160	280
0206/51	Original Teddy, Chocolate Brown, mhr					120	125	135	165	250	250	250	438
0207/10	Grey Teddy Bear, mhr, LE						36	38	38			88	119
0207/12	Original Teddy, Grey, mhr											50	67
0207/14	Grey Teddy Bear, mhr, LE						30					75	101
0207/15	Original Teddy, Grey, mhr											70	94
0207/26	Original Teddy, Grey, mhr, LE							45	45	85	85	85	149
0207/36	Original							62	62	115	115	115	201
0207/41	Original Teddy, Grey, mhr, LE							85	85	160	160	160	280
0208/10	Black Teddy Bear, mhr, LE						36	38	38			88	119
0208/14	Black Teddy Bear, mhr, LE						30					75	125
0208/15	Teddy Bear Scwarz, Meyers Diamond Jubilee, LE 1000, 1989 U												N/P
0209/12	Original Teddy, Black, mhr											50	67
0209/15	Original Teddy, Black, mhr											70	125
0210/12	Original Teddy, Blond, Mini-Mohair										50	50	67
0210/15	Original Teddy, Blond, Mini-Mohair										70	70	125
0210/22	Nimrod Teddy Set, Teddy Roosevelt Comm. Set, mhr, LE 10,000 U				1100							275	550
0211/10	Original Teddy, Rose, LE 8000											60	81
0211/12	Original Teddy, Rose, mhr											50	67
0211/15	Original Teddy, Rose, mhr											70	94
0211/26	Valentine Bear, mhr, 1984					45	48					135	182
0211/36	Valentine Bear, mhr W					60	64					175	236
0212/10	Original Teddy, Cream, mhr, LE						38	38				82	111
0213/10	Original Teddy, Cinnamon, mhr, LE						38	38				82	111
0214/10	Original Teddy, Gold, mhr, LE						38	38				82	111
0215/35	Dormy Bear	60	67	68	68							150	168

Steiff #	Description	1980-1981	1981-1982	1982-1983	1983-1984	1984-1985	1985-1986	1986	1987	1988	1989	1990	Current
0217/34	Dorma Bear		65	66	66	66	66	70				145	162
0218/14	Gieng-Ling Panda, Hobby Center Toys, LE 1000, 1988 U												400
0218/16	Bear		28	28	28	28						60	67
0220/30	Orsi Bear	48	54	55	55							120	150
0223/20	Bruno Bear, Jointed, mhr, LE U			60	60	62	62	62				135	250
0224/35	Petsy Soft											93	104
0225/27	Baby Ophelia with Tutu, mhr, LE, 1988 U									140	140	140	200
0225/42	Ophelia Bear, Jointed, mhr, LE, 1984 U					150	159	169	1100	275	275	275	395
0226/28	Growling Bear											100	135
0227/33	Schnuffy Bear Dressed, 1907 Rep, mhr, LE, 1987 U								1100	275	275		379
0228/33	Growling Bear, mhr								90	125	125	125	169
0228/38	Growling Bear, mhr							125	165	165	165		223
0228/48	Growling Bear, mhr								195	250	250	250	338
0230/20	Teddy Petsy, Rust					39	39					69	77
0230/28	Teddy Petsy, Rust					50	50	53	64	95	95	63	71
0230/35	Teddy Petsy, Rust					70	70	75	90	130	130	85	95
0230/45	Teddy Petsy, Rust					100	100	105	140	190	190	120	134
0233/20	Teddy Petsy, Blonde					39	39	41	41			65	73
0233/28	Teddy Petsy, Blonde					50	50	53	65	95	95	63	71
0233/35	Teddy Petsy, Blonde					70	70	75	90	130	130	85	95
0233/45	Teddy Petsy, Blonde					100	100	105	140	190	190	120	134
0233/80	Teddy Petsy, Blonde						400	425	4100	4100		600	672
0235/20	Teddy Petsy, Cream					39	39	41	41			65	73
0235/28	Teddy Petsy, Cream					50	50	53	65	95	95	63	71
0235/35	Teddy Petsy, Cream					70	70	75	90	130	130	85	95
0235/45	Teddy Petsy, Cream					100	100	105	140	190	190	120	134
0236/28	Petsy Teddy, Augbergine											62	69
0237/20	S-Soft Teddy, Beige, Jointed, mhr, LE					40						90	101
0237/28	Petsy Teddy, Blackberry											62	140
0237/28	S-Soft Teddy, Beige, Jointed, mhr, LE					55	59	62	62			125	140
0237/35	S-Soft Teddy, Beige, Jointed, mhr, LE					75	79	85	85			165	185
0237/45	S-Soft Teddy, Beige, Jointed, mhr, LE					110	115	115	115			245	274
0238/35	Petsy Teddy											85	95
0240/28	Petsy Panda							60	72	110	110	68	76
0240/35	Petsy Panda							80	96	150	150	150	168
0240/45	Petsy Panda							115	140	200	200		224
0243/32	Gold Bear w/Red Ribbon, mhr, WDW, LE, 1000, only 500 produced, 1988 U									95			750
0244/35	Petsy Bear, White, WDW, LE 1000, 1989 U										115		500
0245/32	Margaret Strong Bear, Grey mhr, WDW, LE 1000, 1990 U											125	400
0245/40	Passport Bear, mhr, LE, 1985 W						110	115	140	210		225	304
0245/60	Margaret Strong Bear, WDW, LE 10, 1989 U												N/P
0245/80	Margaret Strong Bear, WDW, LE 1, 1989 U												N/P
0245/80	Petsy, 80cm, WDW, LE 1, 1990 U												N/P
0245/99	Margaret Strong Bear, WDW, LE 1, 1989 U												N/P
0245/99	Petsy, 99cm, WDW, LE 1, 1990 U												N/P
0246/32	Mickey Bear, 32 cm, WDW, LE 1500, 1991 U												650
0246/60	Mickey Bear, WDW, LE 20, 1991 U												2000
0246/80	Mickey Bear, WDW, LE 1, 1991 U												N/P
0246/80	Teddy Baby, Charcoal, WDW, LE 1, 1990 U											10350	N/P
0246/99	Mickey Bear, WDW, LE 1, 1991 U												N/P
0251/34	Berlin Bear, mhr, LE, 1985 U						110	115	115			210	275
0255/35	Clifford Berryman Bear, mhr, LE								170	225	225		300
0260/25	Jackie Bear Rose, Doll House Southern Bear, LE 1000, 1990 U												273
0270/28	Teddy Bear Bride, 1986 W							100	125	175		180	202
027055	Ranch Bear 35, Polo, Ralph Lauren, NY, LE 3,500, 1994 U												450
027062	Preppy Bear 35, Polo, Ralph Lauren, NY, 1994 U												350
027079	Chairman II Bear 43, Polo, Ralph Lauren, LE 1,500, 1994 U												800
027086	Varsity Bear 35, Polo, Ralph Lauren, NY, LE 3,500, 1994 U												350
027093	Producer Bear 43, Polo, Ralph Lauren, NY, LE 1,500, 1994 U												800

Steiff #	Description	1980-1981	1981-1982	1982-1983	1983-1984	1984-1985	1985-1986	1986	1987	1988	1989	1990	Current
0271/28	Teddy Bear Groom, 1986 **W**							100	125			180	202
0275/28	Teddy/Dr							100	125	175		175	196
0276/28	Teddy Bear with Dirndl, 1986 **W**												225
0276/28	Teddy Dressed with Lederhosen, mhr, 1986 **W**							100	125	175	175	175	196
0277/28	Hans, Marshall Fields, 1985 **U**												300
0278/28	Helga, Marshall Fields, 1985 **U**												300
0280/28	Teddy Dressed as a Sailor Boy, mhr, 1986 **W**							100	125	175	175	175	196
0281/28	Teddy Dressed as a Sailor Girl, mhr, 1986 **W**							100	125	175	175	175	196
0283/28	Teddy Dressed w/Black Forest Outfit, mhr, 1987 **W**								150	150		165	185
0284/28	Teddy Dressed w/Farmer Outfit, mhr, 1987 **W**								150	150		165	185
0285/29	Golden Gate Bear, FAO Schwarz/ San Francisco, LE 2000, 1989 **U**												600
0290/32	Toddel	43	50	51								100	112
0291/26	Harrods Musical Bear 1909, LE 2000, 1989 **E**												375
0293/32	California Musical Honey Bear, LE 2000, 1989 **U**												275
0294/42	Harrods Musical Bear 1920, Elise von Beethoven, LE 2000, 1991 **E**												N/P
0296/38	Hamleys Tobias mit musikwerk, LE 2000, 1992 **E**												350
0302/30	Zotty	60	67	70	70	70	70					110	123
0302/40	Zotty	85	95	98	98	98	98					160	179
0302/50	Zotty	125	140	145	145	145	145	155				230	258
0305/22	Zotty	34	40	41								200	224
0305/30	Zotty Bear						63	67	81	135	135	85	95
0305/32	Zotty, mhr	46	50	55								270	302
0305/40	Zotty Bear						95	100	125	200	200	125	140
0305/45	Zotty, mhr	98	115	120								410	459
0305/50	Zotty Bear						130	140	170	250	250	150	168
0310/19	Buddha Bear, mhr				40	40	43					130	195
0312/30	Minky Zotty									135	135	89	100
0312/40	Minky Zotty									200	200	130	151
0312/50	Minky Zotty									250	250	155	174
0318/32	Molly Minky										115	77	86
0318/42	Molly Minky										160	160	179
0320/55	Molly Teddy		115	120								230	258
0320/65	Molly Teddy		160	165	165	165	165	175	210	265	265	165	200
0321/22	Molly Teddy, Champagne									65	65	42	47
0321/32	Molly Teddy, Champagne									115	115	70	78
0321/55	Molly Teddy, Champagne				100	100	100	105	140	200	200	125	140
0322/22	Molly Teddy, Cream									65	65	42	47
0322/32	Molly Teddy, Cream									115	115	70	78
0322/40	Molly Teddy, Cream					80	80	85	110	150	150	96	108
0323/50	Super Molly Teddy, Standing							395	525			539	604
0323/60	Molly Teddy, Brown											175	196
0323/65	Molly Panda		158	165	165							295	330
0324/60	Super Molly Teddy, Lying								395	525		525	588
0324/75	Molly Teddy											265	297
0326/32	Molly Panda, B/W	52	58	60	60	60	60	65	78	110	110	110	123
0326/45	Molly Panda, B/W	93	100	110	110	110	110	115	140	190		190	213
0327/32	Molly Panda, Brown	48	54									130	146
0327/45	Molly Panda, Brown	90	100									220	246
0327/85	Standing Bear on 4 Legs								2963		4335	3895	4362
0328/99	Bear Standing on 2 Legs								2963		4335	3895	4362
0329/08	Brown Bear Standing on 4 Legs								2315			2500	3200
0329/16	Brown Bear Standing								2315			2500	3200
0330/32	Molly Bear	36	40	41	41	45	45	48	58	95	95	95	106
0330/45	Molly Bear	84	97	100	100	100	100	105	125	160		175	196
0330/70	Molly Bear	190	250	265	265	265						410	459
0331/22	Molly Koala	37	40									76	85
0331/33	Molly Bear, Sitting									185	185	185	207
0331/40	Molly Koala	68	68									125	140
0332/33	Molly Dog										175	175	196
0332/45	Molly Petsy		95	98	98	98						180	202
0333/33	Molly Elephant, Sitting									185	185	185	207
0333/35	Molly Grizzly		95	98	98							180	202
0333/55	Molly Grizzly		170	175								330	370
0334/33	Molly Cat										175	175	196
0334/45	Molly Polar Bear		95	98	98							180	202

Steiff #	Description	1980-1981	1981-1982	1982-1983	1983-1984	1984-1985	1985-1986	1986	1987	1988	1989	1990	Current
0334/55	Molly Polar Bear		140	145								270	302
0335/55	Molly Donkey		95	98	98	98	98	105	125	175		180	202
0335/80	Molly Donkey	185	250									370	414
0336/55	Molly Pony		95	98								198	222
0337/50	Schnauzer	138	170									270	302
0338/34	Molly Rabbit		69	70	70	70						125	140
0338/35	Molly Chow	63	76									115	129
0338/60	Molly Chow	145	175									230	258
0340/35	Molly Husky	72	89									115	129
0340/60	Molly Husky	145	175									230	258
0341/40	Super Molly Bear				90	90	90	95	125	170	170	170	190
0341/65	Super Molly Bear				185	185	185	195	250	350	350	350	392
0341/90	Super Molly Bear				300	300	300	320	400	600	600	600	672
0341/98	Super M				450	450	450	475	575			785	879
0341/99	Super Molly Bear	600	680	700	700							920	1030
0342/40	S-Molly St. Bernard					80	80					130	146
0342/60	S-Molly St. Bernard					150	150					245	274
0342/80	S-Molly St. Bernard					275	275	295				450	504
0342/98	S-Molly St. Bernard					400	400	425				660	739
0342/99	Super Molly Dog		680	700	700							1050	1176
0343/25	Molly Bear										150	97	109
0343/32	Molly Bear										220	145	498
0343/40	Molly Bear										325	205	230
0343/50	Molly Bello Dog									185	185	185	207
0343/80	Super Molly Seal	225	270	275	275							390	437
0344/99	S Molly Elephant					600	600	650				900	1008
0345/25	Molly Woodchuck		43	43	43	43						80	90
0345/35	Molly Bear										205	135	151
0345/45	Molly Bear										290	185	207
0345/50	Molly Lynx	140	175									230	258
0345/60	Molly Bear										350	230	258
0345/80	Molly Bear										575	375	420
0346/30	Molly Groundhog	48	57	58	58	58	58	61	75	115		120	134
0347/55	Fox		148	150	150	150	150	160	195			280	314
0347/55	Molly Bear, Brown											165	185
0348/22	Molly Raccoon	42	52	53								110	123
0350/45	Molly Dog		95	98	98	98						180	202
0350/65	Molly Dog		157	160	160							295	330
0355/35	Molly Polar Bear, Sitting											135	151
0360/45	Molly Pig		95	98	98	98	98	105	125	175		180	201
0361/90	Super Molly Pig				275	275	275	295	375	525	525	310	347
0363/40	Molly Zicky Goat											115	129
0363/50	Molly Zicky Goat											150	168
0365/40	Molly Pony, Brown								125		125	77	86
0365/50	Molly Pony								175	235		235	263
0365/99	Super Molly Cow				400	400	400					700	784
0366/99	Super Molly Pony				400	400	400	425				700	784
0367/40	Molly Pony, Black										125	125	140
0367/99	Super Molly Donkey				400	400	400	425	425			700	784
0368/45	Molly Baby Lion										195	125	140
0370/30	Molly Leo Lion							70	85	125	135	87	97
0370/40	Molly Lamb		74	76	76	76						140	157
0370/70	Molly Leo Lion								295	400	400	250	280
0371/30	Molly Baby Lion											110	123
0375/45	Lion		175	180	180	180	180	195				342	383
0376/45	Molly Young Tiger										195	125	140
0376/60	Molly Young Tiger										330	330	370
0378/60	Molly Tiger									230	230	230	258
0380/28	Baloo Bear	46	51									225	252
0380/30	Molly Tiger Taky							70	85	125	135	87	97
0381/25	Bagheera Panther	48	53	53								225	252
0381/50	Super Molly Lion, Standing								280	380	380	380	426
0382/22	Baby Hathi Elephant	43	48									225	252
0382/60	Super Molly Lion, Lying								260	360	360	360	403
0383/22	King Louis Chimp	48	53	53								225	252
0385/75	Molly Puma				130	130				250		250	280
0385/98	Molly Puma						295					445	498

Steiff #	Description	1980-1981	1981-1982	1982-1983	1983-1984	1984-1985	1985-1986	1986	1987	1988	1989	1990	Current
0387/75	Molly Panther					130	130	140	170	250	250	250	280
0387/98	Molly Panther						295	310			445		498
0390/40	Molly Leopard									160	160	105	118
0390/50	Molly Leopard								175	235	235	235	263
0405/40	Molly Camel									230	230	125	140
0405/60	Molly Camel									315	315	315	353
0409/19	Bear, Standing St 69"	2493	2593									4700	5264
0410/50	Bear on Wheels	200										685	1201
0411/40	Molly Zebra									125	125	125	140
0417/60	Brown Bear Cub		175	180	180							340	381
0420/40	Molly Moose										230	145	162
0438/70	Super Molly Panda						195	205	250			320	358
0438/98	Super Molly Panda						425	450	450			695	778
0439/07	Panda					150							600
0439/13	Panda					425							1300
0440/99	Goat										3550	3000	3360
0445/60	Little Goat										1000	575	644
0446/60	Little Goat										1000	575	644
0450/99	Donkey										3975	3995	4474
0453/75	Little Donkey										2750	2000	2240
0460/45	Molly Husky										195	125	140
0460/60	Molly Husky										330	330	370
0467/23	Polar Bear, White	50	57	58								95	106
0468/60	Polar Bear Cub		175	180	180							340	381
0470/99	Polar Bear			2565	2565							4600	5152
0472/99	Polar Bear			945	945	945	945	1195			1843	1700	1904
0477/60	Panda Bear Cub		188	195	195							345	386
0500/30	Bamboo Monkey, Light Brown								80	110		110	123
0500/45	Bamboo Monkey, Light Brown								110	150		150	168
0500/55	Bamboo Monkey, Light Brown								175	240		240	269
0505/18	Elephant	38	42	43	43							75	84
0505/30	Bamboo Monkey, Cream								80	110		110	123
0505/45	Bamboo Monkey, Cream								110	150		150	168
0505/55	Bamboo Monkey, Cream								175	240		240	269
0520/50	Bongo Orang., Rust								185	250	250	250	280
0525/50	Bongo Orang., Cream								185	250	250	250	280
0535/32	Baby Gorilla											81	91
0540/45	Gora Gorilla								185	250	250	150	168
0540/60	Gora Gorilla								250	330	330	185	207
0544/99	Gora Gorilla										1800	2000	2240
0595/35	Mammouth, Trampy											105	118
0609/16	Camel, Standing St 63"	2385	2495	2700	2778	2778			3334		4315	3895	4362
0710/35	Kangaroo/Baby	45	50	53	57	57	57	60				85	95
0755/28	Giraffe	30	39	39	39	45	45	48				60	67
0755/40	Giraffe	42	50	51	52	56	56	59				80	90
0755/60	Giraffe	70	89	90	90	90	90					135	151
0759/15	Giraffe St 60", mhr	1377	1450	1557	1557	1557	1557		1945		2593	2350	2632
0759/24	Giraffe St 96", mhr	2340	2500	2655	2655	2655	2655		3334		4769	4350	4872
0800/20	Lion	38	42									75	84
0805/18	Lion, Standing	28										54	60
0805/26	Lion, Standing	39	48									75	84
0805/99	Lion, Standing										5694	6000	6900
0807/99	Lioness, Lying										3750	4000	4750
0809/11	Lion, Standing St 42"	2223	2547	2547	2547	2547	2547		2621			4300	4816
0812/16	Rango Lion	38	43	43	43							75	84
0815/15	Sulla Lioness	35	39	40								70	78
0820/16	Wittie Tiger	35	39	40	40							70	78
0822/99	Tiger, Standing St 59"	1800	2000	2210	2210	2210	2210		2778			3975	4200
0825/16	Sigi Leopard	35	39	40	40							70	78
0870/60	Tiger Cub Pascha					155	155	165	200	265	265	265	297
0885/50	Leopard, Lying			105	105	105	105					195	218
0890/40	Leopard Cub	140	160	165	165							295	330
0892/40	Kango Kangaroo with Baby										210	140	157
1150/45	Seal Robby											96	108
1170/16	Walrus									65	65	42	47
1172/80	Walrus									375	375	375	420
1172/99	Walrus									1600	1600	1600	1792

Key: W = World Wide • U = USA • E = England • G = Germany • WDW = Walt Disney World • DL = Disneyland • N/P = No prices available

Steiff #	Description	1980-1981	1981-1982	1982-1983	1983-1984	1984-1985	1985-1986	1986	1987	1988	1989	1990	Current
1174/55	Walrus									215		215	255
1175/14	Seal	31	35	36	36	36	36					60	67
1175/20	Seal	49	59	60								95	106
1178/14	Seal	31	38	38	38	38	38					60	67
1179/04	Sealion Cub	125	140	145								235	263
1210/25	Bear, Standing											81	91
1212/25	Bear, Sitting											89	100
1215/25	Bear, Lying											89	100
1220/25	Polar Bear, Standing											81	91
1222/25	Polar Bear, Sitting											89	100
1225/25	Polar Bear, Lying											89	100
1232/25	Mohair Soft Schwarzbear (Black Bear Cup), FAO Schwarz, LE 2000, 1990 U												250
1305/09	Jumbo Elephant, Mini-Mohair										50	50	55
1305/12	Jumbo Elephant, Mini-Mohair										70	70	78
1306/12	Waldi Hound, Tan, mhr											70	78
1307/12	Kitty Cat, White, mhr											70	78
1308/12	Mouse Fiep, Grey, mhr											60	67
1310/12	Mouse Fiep, White, mhr											60	67
1311/12	Fox Fuzzy											70	78
1312/12	Possy Squirrel, mhr											70	78
1313/12	Hound Waldi, Brown, mhr											70	78
1314/12	Cat Kitty, Black, mhr											70	78
1350/10	Timmy Rabbit, Mini-Mohair										50	50	55
1350/12	Timmy Rabbit, Mini-Mohair										70	70	78
1444/12	Browny Bear						23	24	30	50	50	32	36
1445/12	Browny Bear	17	20	21	23	29						42	47
1446/11	Koala Bear		22	23	23	23	23	25	30	42	42	45	50
1447/17	Polar Bear		25	26	26							50	56
1448/13	Kango Kangaroo										50	50	56
1450/12	Jumbo Elephant	17	20	21	23	29						39	45
1451/09	Rhino	16	18	19	19							39	44
1451/12	Jumbo Elephant						23	24	30	50	50	32	36
1453/14	Hockey Dromedary	17	20	21	23							39	44
1453/15	Trampy Camel						23	24	30	50		50	56
1456/09	Nosy Rhino						23	24	30	50		50	56
1457/14	Elk	25	28	28								60	67
1458/12	Bison	22	24	25								50	56
1460/13	Lion	17	20	21	23	31						39	44
1461/12	Leo Lion						23	24	30	50	50	32	36
1463/18	Gaty Crocodile						27	29	35	55	55	55	62
1464/12	Fox Woodland Animal						25	34	50		50	56
1465/10	Fox	19	21	22	22	24	24	26	32			45	50
1466/12	Squirrel Woodland Animal						25	36	50	50	32	36
1467/10	Squirrel	17	19	20	20	20	20					39	44
1468/10	Wild Boar	19	21	21	21	21	21	22	27	40		39	44
1470/12	Paddy Beaver		20	21	21	21	21	22	27	40	40	40	45
1472/07	Dolphin	11	14	14	14	14	14	15	18	30	30	30	34
1473/09	Seal	13	16	17	18	18	18	19	23	40	40	40	45
1474/10	Walrus	16	17	18	18	18						39	44
1476/12	Marmot Woodland Animal							25	34	50	50	50	56
1480/12	Ermine Woodland Animal							25	34			50	56
1493/13	Susi Cat, Grey			23	23	23	23	25	30	45		45	50
1493/14	Cat, Black			23	23	23						45	50
1495/10	Kitty Cat	14	16	17								39	44
1496/10	Black Tom Cat	22	24	25	25	25						52	58
1500/09	Hoppy, Lying, Brown	14	17	18	18							32	36
1500/13	Hoppy, Beige					25	25	27	33			35	39
1501/09	Hoppy, Lying, Grey	14	17	18	18							32	36
1501/13	Hoppy, Grey					25	25	27	33			35	39
1502/10	Manni, Sitting, Brown	14	17									32	36
1502/15	Manni, Beige					25	25	27	33			35	39
1503/10	Manni, Sitting, Grey	14	17									45	50
1503/15	Manni, Grey					25	25	27	33			35	39
1505/10	Piggy Pig		22	23	23	23	23	25	30	45	45	30	33
1510/14	Donkey	17	19	21	23	29	29					45	50
1512/16	Ossi, Zebra			25	26	26	26					48	54

Steiff #	Description	1980-1981	1981-1982	1982-1983	1983-1984	1984-1985	1985-1986	1986	1987	1988	1989	1990	Current
1516/14	Pony	17	20	21	23	17	17	29				34	38
1518/11	Lamb	13	16	17	17	17	17	18	22			40	45
1520/11	Sheep, B/W	13	16	17	17	17	17	18	22			40	45
1522/14	Horse								38	58	58	37	41
1523/20	Shepherd and His Flock	69	80									320	358
1524/12	Cow								38	58	58	58	64
1525/08	Pig								34	50	50	50	56
1526/11	Dog	13	15									34	38
1526/12	Brown Baby Goat								36	50	55	55	62
1527/12	White Baby Lamb								36	50	55	55	62
1528/11	Fox Terrier	15	18	19	19	27	27					36	40
1530/12	Schnauzer	17	19									40	45
1532/12	Poodle, Black	18	20	21	21	21						40	45
1533/12	Poodle, White	18	20	21	21	21						40	45
1540/20	Xorry Fox, Lying							40	48	70	70	46	52
1542/35	Red Fox, Sleeping	67	75	76	76	76	76	80	96	120	120	74	83
1543/35	Raccoon, Sleeping	67	67									175	196
1544/35	Fox, Sleeping, Beige	70	78	79	79							175	196
1548/25	Fuzzy Fox										115	78	87
1550/12	Owl Woodland Animal							25	30	50	50	31	35
1670/06	Hedgehog, Lying, mhr	4	5	5	6	6	6	7	8	14	14	14	15
1670/10	Hedgehog	9	10	13	14	16	16					44	49
1670/17	Hedgehog, Lying, mhr	17	21	23	25	28	28					75	84
1675/12	Joggi Hedgehog						18	19	23	40	40	25	28
1675/18	Joggi Hedgehog						24	25	30	50	50	50	56
1675/35	Hedgehog Joggi											93	104
1675/45	Super Joggi Hedgehog							60	145	220		220	246
1675/70	Super Joggi Hedgehog							295	360	500		500	560
1677/14	Joggi Hedgehog, Begging						24	25	30	50	50	32	36
1677/20	Hedgehog Joggi											46	52
1677/50	Hedgehog									350		350	392
1680/12	Hedgehog, Begging, mhr	16	20	21	22	22	22					70	78
1820/14	Fawn	24	26	27	27							58	65
1830/40	Deer, Standing	85	95	98								155	174
1831/20	Fawn, Lying									75	75	48	54
1831/38	Fawn, Lying	55	63	64	64	64	64	68	82	100	100	100	111
1834/40	Lamb	66										120	134
1835/22	Fawn, Standing									100	100	100	111
1837/30	Doe, Lying									120	120	120	134
1838/30	Roebuck, Standing									145	145	145	162
1840/26	Diggy Badger							60	72	110		115	129
1840/36	Diggy Badger							80	100	150		165	185
2015/24	Squirrel									135	135	86	96
2025/18	Chipmunk Chippy										90	60	67
2030/20	Squirrel	31	37	38						75		58	65
2032/25	Possy Squirrel			41	41	41	41	44				75	84
2040/12	Perri Squirrel, mhr	18	22	23	23							85	95
2040/17	Perri Squirrel, mhr	22										110	123
2040/25	Putsi Otter, Standing								85	110		115	129
2042/24	Marmot Piff, Grey/Brown											63	71
2045/25	Putsi Otter, Sitting								85	110		115	129
2050/25	Raggy Raccoon, Standing								95	125	125	81	91
2055/35	Raggy Raccoon, Sitting								145	195	195	120	134
2060/20	Raggy Ringel Racoon								65	90	90	57	64
2070/25	Piff Marmot, Standing								85	110	110	110	123
2080/35	Skunk										160	105	118
2121/18	Beaver	29										55	62
2125/20	Nagy Beaver		34	35	35	35	35	37	37			65	73
2150/12	Goldy Hamster							24	25	30	50	50	56
2150/16	Goldy Hamster							29	31	38	62	65	73
2150/50	Super Goldy Hamster							295	310	310	310	310	347
2155/12	Hamster	17	20	21	21	21						34	38
2155/17	Hamster	22	27	27	27	27						42	47
2160/20	Otty Otter			30								55	62
2170/10	Mouse, White	11	13	14	14	14	14	15	18	30	30	30	34
2171/10	Mouse, Grey	11	13	14	14	14	14	15	18	30	30	30	34
2180/12	Mole/Shovel, mhr	11	14	18	19	19	19	20	24	40		45	50

Steiff #	Description	1980-1981	1981-1982	1982-1983	1983-1984	1984-1985	1985-1986	1986	1987	1988	1989	1990	Current
2180/15	Maxi Mole	22	29	30	30	30	30					45	50
2205/12	Woodchuck	24	26	27	27	27	27					49	55
2251/18	Guinea Pig Ginny											37	41
2251/22	Guinea Pig Ginny											44	49
2252/10	Guinea Pig	19	21	22	22	22	22	23	28	40		42	47
2254/15	Guinea Pig					29	29	31				48	54
2255/15	Guinea Pig, Mama	24	30									49	55
2256/15	Guinea Pig, Papa	24	30	31	31							48	54
2270/22	Mouse Pieps, Grey											66	74
2270/25	Otter	32	32									65	73
2270/35	Otter	54										95	106
2275/22	Mouse Pieps, White											66	74
2300/10	Fish, Blue, mhr	8	9									40	45
2301/10	Fish, Gold, mhr	8	9									40	45
2311/25	Fish, Green	28										52	58
2320/25	Dolphin	23	26	27	27							44	49
2320/35	Dolphin	28	33	33	33							55	62
2322/35	Finny Dolphin								57	75		75	84
2322/50	Finny Dolphin								89	120		120	134
2322/99	Finny Dolphin								450	600		600	672
2370/08	Frog, Sitting	17	20	21	21	24	24	26	32			39	44
2380/32	Frog, Dangling	29	32	32	32	32						57	64
2455/14	Turtle	19	23	24	24	24						85	95
2455/22	Turtle	36										135	151
2460/30	Ladybug/Wheels, mhr	145										445	498
2505/12	Penguin	16	19	19	20	20	20	21	26	37	37	37	41
2505/27	Penguin	35	40	41								70	78
2505/40	Penguin	59	77									115	129
2507/20	Baby Penguin				33	33	33	35	42	70	70	70	78
2507/38	Penguin			72	72	72	72	76	92	135		130	146
2509/09	Penguin St 36"	450	450	450	450	450	450		620		834	850	952
2510/40	Charly Penguin								115	150	150	150	168
2511/26	Paddy Puffin	57	65									115	129
2531/13	Parakeet, Gold/Green	18	22	23	23	23	23					54	60
2534/13	Parakeet, White/Blue	18	22	23	23	23	23	25	30	47	47	47	53
2540/30	Parrot, Red, Studio	76	89	90	90	90	90		130			225	252
2541/30	Parrot, Blue, Studio	76	89	90	90	90	90		130			225	252
2544/30	Lora Parrot, Red								95	125		125	140
2545/30	Cockatoo			90	90	90						180	202
2550/30	Lora Parrot, Green								95	125		165	185
2555/14	Parrot Lori											45	50
2560/14	Tucan Tucky											45	50
2560/20	Tucky Tucan										105	105	118
2565/14	Pelican Peli											45	50
2565/20	Peli Pelican										105	105	118
2570/14	Penguin Peggy											45	50
2580/14	Raven Hucky											45	50
2590/50	Owl		295									475	532
2591/22	Owlet		50	50	50	50	50	53	65	90	90	90	101
2592/25	Baby Owl Wiggy											59	66
2593/28	Screech Owl		97	99	99	99	99	105	125	190		195	218
2603/28	Woodpecker, Spotted	82	82									158	177
2604/28	Woodpecker, Green	82	82									158	177
2605/20	Kingfisher 8"	82	82									158	177
2606/50	Heron 20"	190	190	195	195	195						360	403
2608/50	Stork 20"	200	200	200	200	200						380	426
2612/20	Swan, White				40	40	40					75	84
2615/28	Falcon, Studio	85	97	99	99	99	99	105	125	195		200	224
2620/99	Peacock, Studio	800	950	1000	1000	1000	1000		1400	1600	1963	1700	1904
2621/80	Peacock, Studio	750	900	900	1000							1500	1680
2622/18	Wittie Eagle Owl								55	75	75	75	84
2622/24	Wittie Eagle Owl								89	120		120	134
2622/40	Pheasant	260	295	295	295							495	554
2623/40	Golden Pheasant	275	300	315	315							550	616
2625/15	Owl	26	30	31	31	31	31	33	40			58	65
2625/25	Owl	41	50	50	50							80	90
2650/23	Young Wild Boar									120		120	134

Steiff #	Description	1980-1981	1981-1982	1982-1983	1983-1984	1984-1985	1985-1986	1986	1987	1988	1989	1990	Current
2655/28	Young Wild Boar Wutzi											100	111
2655/40	Young Wild Boar Wutzi											135	151
2660/20	Bora Wild Boar								57	75		75	84
2660/30	Bora Wild Boar								89	120		120	134
2675/15	Wild Boar	33	39	39	39	39	39					65	73
2675/20	Wild Boar			50	52	65	65					90	101
2677/30	Baby Boar			81	81	81	81	86				140	157
2678/50	Wild Boar St		230	235	235	235						425	476
2690/32	Scottish Highland Bull									180	180	180	202
2695/35	Buffalo									200	200	200	224
2710/28	Cat Minka, Standing											92	103
2715/35	Cat Minka, Lying											84	94
2720/22	Cat, Grey	37	37									70	78
2725/22	Cat, Spotted	37	45									70	78
2726/17	Sissi Cat	35	38	39	39	39	39	41	50	75	75	47	53
2726/22	Sissi Cat	45	49	50	50	50	50	53	65	95		95	106
2728/17	Lizzy Cat	35	38	39	39	39	39	41	50	75	75	75	84
2728/22	Lizzy Cat	45	49	50	50	50	50	53	65	95		95	106
2732/17	Tabby	35	38	39	39							75	84
2735/16	Sulla Cat, Cream					38	38	40				75	84
2735/26	Sulla Cat, Cream					58	58	61				105	118
2736/16	Sulla Cat, Grey					38	38	40	48	75		75	84
2736/26	Sulla Cat, Grey					58	58	61	75	105		105	118
2738/16	Dossy Cat, Black					38	38	40	48	75	75	75	84
2738/26	Dossy Cat, Black					58	58	61	75	105	105	105	118
2740/25	Siamese		57	63	64	64							120
2742/23	Cat								120	120		200	224
2745/30	Cat, Lying				75	75						130	146
2750/22	Ringel Cat, Lying		50	50	50							90	101
2752/26	Persian Cat, Grey			62	63	63	63					110	123
2752/35	Persian Cat, Grey			110	110	110						195	218
2753/26	Angora Cat, White			62	63	63	63					110	123
2754/25	Minou Cat, Lying, Cream							70	85	120	120	120	134
2754/40	Minou Cat, Lying, Cream							100	125	175	175	120	134
2755/25	Minou Cat, Lying, Grey							70	85	120		120	134
2755/40	Minou Cat, Lying, Grey							100	125	175		175	196
2756/25	Minou Cat, Lying, Black							70	85	120	120	120	134
2756/40	Minou Cat, Lying, Black							100	125	175		175	196
2757/25	Minou Cat, Striped								92	120	120	120	134
2757/40	Minou Cat, Striped								130	175	175	175	196
2758/40	Cat									175	175	175	196
2877/30	Jr. Petsy			74	74	74						130	146
2881/35	Fox, Crouching	70	85									140	157
2882/25	Jr. Rabbit, Lying	38	38									75	84
2882/35	Jr. Fox Terrier			81	89	89	89	95				165	185
2882/35	Jr. Rabbit, Lying		57	57									110
2883/30	Jr. Schnauzer, Sitting	67										120	134
2883/35	Jr. Charly Dog			81	81	81	81	86				140	157
2884/26	Jr. Cockie		75	75	75							125	140
2884/30	Jr. Schnauzer, Lying	67										120	134
2885/28	Dog, Sitting	59	70									110	123
2886/28	Dog, Lying	59	70									110	123
2887/26	Swiss Mtn Dog			75	75							140	157
2888/35	St. Bernard	90	110	115	115							170	190
2890/22	Jr. Pekinese			53	53	53	53					95	106
2892/28	Jr. Fuzzy Fox		79	80	80							150	168
2893/30	Jr. Scotch Terrier			74	74	74						135	151
2897/30	Jr. Leo Lion Cub			91	95	95	95	100	100	180	180	180	202
2910/12	Snuffy Rabbit, Brown	15	19	19								32	36
2910/18	Snuffy Rabbit, Brown	19	24	24								38	43
2911/12	Snuffy Rabbit, Grey	15	19	19								32	36
2911/18	Snuffy Rabbit, Grey	19	24	24								38	43
2912/18	Snuffy Elephant								50	65		65	73
2914/18	Snuffy Lion								55	75	75	75	84
2916/16	Snuffy Fox								50	67	67	67	75
2918/18	Snuffy Pig								50	66	66	66	74
2920/16	Snuffy Bear				29	29	29	31	38			50	56

Steiff #	Description	1980-1981	1981-1982	1982-1983	1983-1984	1984-1985	1985-1986	1986	1987	1988	1989	1990	Current
2921/16	Snuffy Bear								42	56		60	67
2923/16	Snuffy Dog				32	32	32	34	42	62		62	69
2926/16	Snuffy Cat				32	32	32					55	62
2927/16	Snuffy Cat				32	32	32					55	62
2928/16	Snuffy Cat								50	65	65	42	47
2931/16	Snuffy, Beige/White				29	29	29	30	38	55		55	62
2932/16	Snuffy, Caramel				29	29	29	30	38	55		55	62
2933/16	Snuffy, Dark Brown				29	29	29	30	38	55		55	62
2945/25	Rabbit	37	47	48								70	78
2947/35	Ossi, Standing	38	42									70	78
2950/32	Mummy Rabbit, Begging, Beige									120	125	125	140
2955/18	Winni, Grey, Sitting	30	33									60	67
2955/32	Mummy Rabbit, Begging, Grey									120	125	125	140
2956/16	Hoppel Rabbit											37	41
2956/18	Winni, Brown, Sitting	30	33									60	67
2957/13	Hoppel, Grey	33	37	37	37							62	69
2957/22	Hoppel Rabbit											63	71
2958/13	Poppel, Beige	33	37	37	37							62	69
2958/25	Hoppel Rabbit											63	71
2960/22	Sonny, Grey	45	50	51	51	51	51	54	65			86	96
2961/22	Ronny, Beige	45	50	51	51	51	51	54	65			86	96
2962/16	Mummy, Grey	32	35	36	36							61	68
2962/25	Poppel Rabbit											63	71
2963/16	Pummy, Beige	32	35	36	36							60	67
2965/20	Rabbit, Sitting	29	35	35								46	52
2965/25	Rabbit, Sitting	38	50									70	78
2968/35	Snobby Rabbit				72	72	72	76	95			120	134
2970/23	B/W, Sp	43	51	52	52	52						85	90
2970/30	B/W, Spotted	72	89	90	90							150	168
2972/40	Dormy Rabbit, Lying									165	175	110	123
2974/16	Dormili Rabbit							35	50	73	75	47	53
2975/25	Dormy Rabbit						67	71	86	120	125	75	84
2977/20	Dormili Rabbit							37	50	75		75	84
2978/35	Dormy Rabbit, Begging								115	160	165	165	185
2982/17	B/W Spottili, Running								55	75	80	80	90
2984/17	B/W Spottili, Sitting								53	73	75	75	84
2985/30	B/W Spotty, Sitting								100	140		140	157
2992/17	Grey & White Spottili, Running								55	75	80	80	90
2994/17	Grey & White Spottili, Sitting								53	73	75	75	84
2995/30	Grey & White Spotty, Sitting								100	140	150	150	168
3020/00	Manni Rabbit Set, 3 pc., 1983, LE						175	175				375	420
3020/10	Manni Rabbit, mhr				35							95	106
3020/30	Manni Rabbit, mhr				75	75	75					175	196
3135/45	Ango	53	65	65								100	112
3141/43	Lulac, Brown, mhr	36	44									135	151
3142/43	Lulac, Grey, mhr	36										135	151
3155/16	Timmy, Brown	23	28	28	28							45	50
3156/16	Timmy, Grey	23	28	28	28							45	50
3205/15	Tulla Duck	23	27	28	28	28	28	30	36			43	48
3210/16	Willa Duck, Green									46	48	48	54
3210/22	Willa Duck, Green									60		60	67
3211/16	Pilla Duck, Blue									46		50	56
3211/22	Pilla Duck, Blue									60		60	67
3215/16	Tulla Duck, Red									46		50	56
3215/22	Tulla Duck, Red									60		60	67
3230/11	Duck Daggi										35	35	39
3232/11	Duck Daggi										35	35	39
3240/16	Duck Waggi											35	39
3240/20	Duck Waggi											48	54
3242/08	Piccy Duck	10	11	11								25	28
3242/11	Piccy Duck	14	16	16								32	36
3243/16	Duck Waggi											35	39
3243/20	Duck Waggi											48	54
3247/26	Swan	57	65	66								140	157
3450/22	Locky Lamb	36	40									72	81
3455/17	Zicky Goat			38	38	38						70	78
3455/56	Zicky Goat			60	60							100	112

Steiff #	Description	1980-1981	1981-1982	1982-1983	1983-1984	1984-1985	1985-1986	1986	1987	1988	1989	1990	Current
3460/20	Rocky Wild Goat			41	43	43						80	90
3460/25	Lamb Lamby										77	77	86
3460/30	Lamb Lamby										95	95	106
3462/22	Lamb Lamby										65	43	48
3464/22	Lamb Lamby, Brown										65	43	48
3475/40	Elbow Puppet-Leopard	74	80	82								140	157
3476/40	Elbow Puppet-Skunk	80	87	88								150	168
3477/50	Elbow Puppet-Raccoon	80	87	88								150	168
3478/50	Elbow Puppet-Puma/Lion	86	94									170	190
3480/40	Elbow Puppet-Rabbit, Grey	58	60	61	65	65	65	69	69			100	112
3480/41	Rabbit, White							69	69			115	129
3481/40	Elbow Puppet-Rabbit, Brown	58	60	61	65	65	65	69				110	123
3483/40	Elbow Puppet-Cat	70	76									135	151
3490/45	Mimic Bear				75	75	75	79	95			165	185
3492/45	Mimic Dog				75	75	75	79	95			120	134
3515/14	Snuffy Fox	19	24									38	43
3515/18	Snuffy Fox	25	32									50	56
3518/14	Snuffy Lion	19	24	24								38	43
3518/18	Snuffy Lion	25	32	32								50	56
3520/12	Snuffy Cat, Beige	17	21	22								36	40
3520/17	Snuffy Cat, Beige	22	28									40	45
3521/12	Snuffy Cat, Grey	17	21	22								36	40
3521/17	Snuffy Cat, Grey	22	28	29								40	45
3605/27	Donkey	39	47									75	84
3710/60	Pony on Wheels	225										675	1181
3740/25	Siamese		57	63	64	64							120
3750/18	Pony, Brown, mhr	24	29									120	134
3760/25	Horse, Brown	57	63	64	65	65	65					110	112
3785/25	Horse, Beige	53	58	59	59							100	112
3790/18	Calf	34	38	38								65	73
3792/25	Cow	57	63	64	64							110	123
3795/27	Calf, Lying			66	72	72	72	76	93			115	129
3810/17	Pig	34	38	38	38	38	38	40	48	70	70	45	65
400919	Ur- Teddy, 20cm, 1926, LE 4000												285
4010/12	Mopsy Dog, mhr	17	20									75	84
401534	Circus Bear, 32cm, 1935, LE 4000												N/P
4026/21	Spaniel Cockie, Sitting											74	83
4028/32	Spaniel Cockie, Lying											88	99
4030/14	Pekinese		40	41	41	43	43					75	84
4035/38	Cocker Spaniel					80	80	85	110	150		150	168
4040/99	St. Bernard Dog	450	615	610	665							1065	1193
4045/35	Boxer				80	80	80	85	105	175	175	175	196
4045/50	Boxer, Lying			130	130	130	130	138	165	250	250	105	118
4048/40	German Shepherd				80	80	80					135	151
4048/50	German Shepherd			130	130	130	130	138	165	250		250	280
4050/80	Shepherd, Standing	665	775	796	796							1200	1344
4052/80	Shepherd, Lying	565	625	639	639							1075	1204
4053/20	German Shepherd Puppy				33	33	33					55	62
4053/23	Shepherd, Puppy	66	74	75	75	75	75					125	140
4055/65	Husky	580	650									995	1114
405891	Teddy Bear, 43cm, 1906, LE 5000												325
406010	Teddy Bear 1907, 70cm, LE 5000, 1993												N/P
406041	Teddy Bear, 65cm, 1908, LE 7000												725
406058	Teddy Bear, 65cm, 1909, LE 5000												875
4060/80	Setter, Standing	520	600									1000	1120
4061/80	Setter, Sitting	520	600	602	602							1100	1232
406225	American Flag Bear 35cm, Polo, Ralph Lauren, NY, LE 3,500, 1992 **U**												425
4065/65	Chow	545	600	602	602	585						1000	1120
406744	Otto Steiff Teddy Bear, 40cm, LE 5000 **U**												345
406805	Teddy Bear, 40cm, 1912, LE 7000												350
4070/55	Schnauzer	245	275	285	285							490	549
407175	Teddy Baby with Teeth, 1929, LE 3000												360
407192	Teddy Bear Rose, 48cm, 1927, LE 7000												350
407512	Teddy Baby Girl, 25cm, 1930, LE 7000												220
407529	Teddy Baby Boy, 25cm, 1930, LE 7000												220
4075/60	Boxer	500	575	575	745	745						1110	1243

Key: W = World Wide • U = USA • E = England • G = Germany • WDW = Walt Disney World • DL = Disneyland • N/P = No prices available

NUMERICAL LISTING

Steiff #	Description	1980-1981	1981-1982	1982-1983	1983-1984	1984-1985	1985-1986	1986	1987	1988	1989	1990	Current
4080/50	Terrier	255	285	285	285	285						490	549
408113	Teddy Baby, Yellow, 15cm, LE 5000												160
408144	Teddy Baby, Yellow, 32cm, LE 5000												250
408335	Panda Bear, 1951, LE 3000												575
4085/28	Terrier	72	79									135	151
4090/40	Collie				80	80	80	85	110			160	179
4121/30	Pomeranian, White	72	80	82	82							135	151
4122/30	Pomeranian, Rust	72	80									135	151
4130/20	Mobby Bobtail Dog, Sitting									80	80	80	90
4132/24	Mobby Bobtail Dog, Standing									125	125	125	140
4140/30	Fox Terrier Treff									145	145	92	103
4142/12	Dachshund	24	26	27	27	30	30	32				45	50
4150/25	Raudi Dachshund, Sand/Grey							75	90	135		135	151
4150/40	Raudi Dachshund, Sand/Grey							100	125	190		190	213
4151/25	Raudi Dachshund, Grey/Brown							75	90	135		135	151
4151/40	Raudi Dachshund, Grey/Brown							100	125	190		190	213
4153/25	Dog Raudi											98	110
4156/26	Poodle, Brown	55	60									105	118
4157/26	Poodle, Black	55	60									105	118
4157/50	Poodle, Standing	255	285	285	285							495	554
4158/50	Poodle, Upright	275	300									540	605
4160/24	Welfo Puppy, Standing								95	125	125	125	140
4160/35	Poodle, Black	67	74									120	134
4161/35	Poodle, White	67	74									120	134
4162/22	Welfo Puppy, Lying								100	135		140	157
4162/35	Poodle, Apricot	67	74									120	134
4165/45	Wolfi Dog, Sitting								225	300		320	358
4167/40	Shepherd Dog Arco, Sitting											135	151
4168/45	Shepherd Dog Arco, Lying											170	190
4180/45	Afgan Dog, Standing								235	315		325	364
4182/40	Afgan Dog, Sitting								175	230		245	274
4184/35	Blacky S. Terrier										160	160	179
4185/35	Whity W.H. Terrier										160	160	179
4192/25	Yorkshire Terrier, Sitting								125	165	165	165	185
420016	Teddy Baby Blue, Steiff Club, LE 7959, 1992 **G**												650
420023	Teddy Clown 1928 Club Edition, World Wide												400
420047	Original Steiff Teddybar 1908 Steiff Aug 1994 Worldwide Steiff Club												N/P
420054	Baby Teddy, 1946, Steiff Club												250
420061	Camel on Wheels, 1930, Steiff Club												725
420801	Sam 28, Steiff Club, LE 4000, 1993/94 **U**												750
4215/21	Fox Terrier	48	52									85	95
4215/30	Fox Terrier	73										135	151
4900/22	Fox	22										42	47
5030/17	Pummy Bear										90	90	101
5030/21	Pummy Bear										115	115	129
5035/17	Pummy Koala Bear										105	105	118
5035/21	Pummy Koala Bear										140	80	90
5060/17	Pummy Rabbit										95	60	67
5060/21	Pummy Rabbit										130	83	92
5063/17	Pummy Rabbit										95	95	106
5063/21	Pummy Rabbit										130	130	146
5067/17	Pummy Rabbit										95	95	106
5067/21	Pummy Rabbit										130	130	146
5250/17	Fox Pummy										100	66	74
5250/21	Fox Pummy										135	88	99
5322/35	Panther, Lying	58	75									110	123
5322/50	Panther, Lying	98										180	202
5340/33	Cosy Elephant, Lying									120		120	134
5350/15	Cosy Jumbo Elephant					39	39	41	52	70	70	70	78
5350/22	Cosy Jumbo Elephant					60	60	64	80	110		110	123
5350/30	Cosy Jumbo Elephant					100	100					165	185
5351/40	Leopard, Lying	76	84	85								140	157
5352/25	Cosy Elephant			58	58							95	106
5352/33	Cosy Bear									110		110	123
5353/25	Cosy Bear, Honey Gold			53	53							95	106
5354/25	Cosy Bear, Dk. Brown			53	53							65	73

Steiff #	Description	1980-1981	1981-1982	1982-1983	1983-1984	1984-1985	1985-1986	1986	1987	1988	1989	1990	Current
5355/26	Cosy Bear		35	35	35	35	35	37	45			95	106
5355/36	Cosy Bear		55	55	55	55	55	58	70			95	106
5357/25	Cosy Panda					67	67	70	90	120		120	134
5358/18	Cosy Koala							45	55	80		80	90
5358/27	Cosy Koala			58	58	58	58					95	106
5358/28	Cosy Koala							70	85	125		125	140
5358/38	Cosy Koala							100	125			160	179
5358/50	Cosy Koala							200	250			320	358
5360/25	Cosy Pony			45	46	46	46					85	95
5360/40	Pony	76	83	85	85	85						135	151
5361/24	Cosy Manni			43	43	43						80	90
5362/24	Cosy Hoppy			43	43	43	43					80	90
5363/16	Cosy Snuffy, Beige			28	28	28	28	30	36			45	50
5364/16	Cosy Snuffy, Caramel			28	28	28	28		36			45	50
5368/33	Cosy Dog									95		95	106
5370/28	Cosy Panther	57	63	63	63	63	63	67	82	110		110	123
5372/33	Cosy Puma		64	65	65	65	65					120	134
5374/17	Cosy Seal					25	25	27	33	45		45	50
5374/35	Cosy Seal			49	49	49	49	52	63	90		90	101
5375/30	Cosy Seal Robby, Grey							45	58	85		85	95
5375/31	Cosy Seal Robby, Beige							45	58	85		85	95
5375/57	Cosy Seal			81	81	81	81					145	162
5376/11	Preppy Duck, Boy						20	21	28	40		40	45
5376/12	Preppy Duck, Girl						20	21	28	40		40	45
5376/50	Cosy Seal		125	126								230	258
5377/12	Cosy Piccy Duck			17	18	18	18					32	36
5378/17	Cosy Daggi Duck			21	22	22	22	23				39	44
5382/43	Cosy Froggy		70									135	151
5384/16	Cosy Froggy Frog							44	53	80	80	52	58
5384/20	Cosy Froggy Frog						44	47	57	57		57	64
5384/28	Cosy Froggy Frog						75	80	96	96		96	108
5384/50	Super Cosy Froggy Frog							325	395	395		445	498
5387/27	Cosy Whale				27	27	27	29	36	55		45	50
5390/30	Cosy Mouse, Blue		42									80	90
5391/30	Cosy Mouse, Violet		42									80	90
5392/15	Cosy Mouse, Olive		22										45
5392/30	Cosy Mouse, Green		42	43	43	43	43					80	90
5393/15	Cosy Mouse, White		22	23	23	23	23					40	45
5393/45	Cosy Fiep Mouse, White								145	190		190	213
5394/15	Cosy Mouse, Grey		22	23	23							40	45
5394/45	Cosy Fiep Mouse, Grey								145	190		190	213
5396/17	Cosy Nagy Beaver							31	40	60	60	60	67
5396/22	Cosy Nagy Beaver							46	65	95		95	106
5397/15	Cosy Hedgehog		20	21	21	21	21					39	44
5397/25	Cosy Joggi Hedgehog		30	30	30	30						55	62
5405/17	Cosy Polar Bear				35	35		37	47	47		47	53
5405/30	Cosy Polar Bear				50	50	50	53	64	95	95	95	106
5410/80	Cosy Dolphin		157									250	280
5414/18	Cosy Piggy Pig						30	32	39	63	63	40	45
5415/28	Cosy Pig			49	52	52	52	55	66	100	95	61	68
5420/19	Cosy Nosy Rhino, Lying									95		95	106
5420/75	Cosy Nosy Rhino, Lying									300		300	336
5420/99	Cosy Nosy Rhino, Lying									1600		1600	1792
5422/20	Cosy Nosy Rhino, Standing									95		95	106
5422/40	Cosy Nosy Rhino, Standing									150		150	168
5432/20	Snail Nelly, Purple									55		55	62
5434/20	Snail Nelly, Brown									55		55	62
5438/25	Dolphin Finny, Ice Blue									53		53	59
5440/16	Cosy Sulla, Cream						40	43	52	52		52	58
5440/22	Cosy Sulla, Cream						50	53	65			65	73
5442/16	Cosy Milla, Blonde						40	43	52			52	58
5442/22	Cosy Milla, Blonde						50	53	65	65		65	73
5445/20	Cosy Poodle Tobby, Stndg, Apricot							50	60	90		90	101
5445/28	Cosy Poodle Tobby, Stndg, Apricot							70	87	135		135	151
5447/20	Cosy Poodle Tobby, Stndg, Black							50	60	90		90	101
5447/25	Cosy Flora Cow											125	140
5447/28	Cosy Poodle Tobby, Stndg, Black							70	87	135		135	151

Steiff #	Description	1980-1981	1981-1982	1982-1983	1983-1984	1984-1985	1985-1986	1986	1987	1988	1989	1990	Current
5450/27	Cosy Gora Monkey		79	80	80							145	162
5452/28	Cosy Poodle Nobby, Lying, Grey							75	90	135		135	151
5457/20	Cosy Dog Bello Standing, Grey							50	60	90		90	101
5457/27	Cosy Bello-Dog					63	63					100	112
5460/35	Cosy Daschund			81	81	81	81					145	162
5463/50	Cosy Basset Dog					125	125	135	165	225		225	252
5465/16	Cosy Lumpi Schnauzer						34	36	44	70		70	78
5465/27	Cosy Lumpi Schnauzer						55	58	71	120		120	134
5466/16	Cosy Lumpi Schnauzer, Lying						36	38	46	75		75	84
5472/20	Cosy Grissy Donkey							44	53	80	80	80	90
5472/28	Cosy Grissy Donkey					66	66	70	87	87		87	97
5473/25	Cosy Lamby							52	71	110		110	123
5473/40	Cosy Lamby							72	115	175		175	196
5474/21	Cosy Lamb					39		41	50	70		70	78
5474/27	Cosy Lamb					60		65	78	115		115	129
5475/20	Cosy Horse Ferdy, Brown							44	53	80	80	50	56
5475/28	Cosy Horse Ferdy					59		62	75	125	125	125	140
5476/20	Cosy Horse Yello, Beige							44	53	80		80	90
5480/22	Cosy Zicky Goat							70		100		110	123
5491/18	Gocki Rooster							58	85	85		85	95
5495/18	Gacki Hen							58	85	85		85	95
5498/10	Cosy Bibi Chick							19	27			30	34
5502/13	Cosy Minni, Sitting, Beige/White									42	44	44	49
5503/13	Cosy Minni, Sitting, Brown/Cream									42	44	44	49
5504/13	Cosy Minni, Sitting, Grey/White									42	44	44	49
5505/13	Cosy Minni, Sitting, Black/White									42	44	44	49
5505/25	Cuddly Bear			50	50							95	106
5507/15	Manni, Begging, Brown/White									44	46	46	52
5508/15	Manni, Begging, Brown/Cream									44		44	49
5511/18	Cosy Snuffy, Crouching, Beige/White									60		60	67
5512/18	Cosy Snuffy, Crouching, Rust/Beige									60		60	67
5513/16	Cosy Bunny, Aubergine											37	41
5514/16	Cosy Bunny, Blackberry											37	41
5520/25	Cat, Grey			50	50	50	50					90	101
5525/25	Rabbit, Brown			50	50	50						92	103
5526/25	Ango, White		50	51	51	51						95	106
5530/25	Cuddly Dog			50	50							90	101
5558/10	Mini Cosy Hedgehog							15	18	28	28	28	31
5565/10	Blue Bird								19	30		32	36
5567/10	Brown Bird								19	30		32	36
5578/11	Penquin								23	30		32	36
5585/15	Blue Dolphin								23	35		35	39
5588/15	Grey Dolphin								23	35		35	39
5600/18	Floppy Bear				36	36	36	38	48	65		65	73
5600/25	Floppy Bear				50	50	50					95	106
5605/18	Floppy Rabbit				36	36	36	38	48	69		69	77
5605/25	Floppy Rabbit				50	50	50		50			85	95
5610/18	Floppy Dog				36	36	38	38	48	70		70	78
5610/25	Floppy Dog				50							85	95
5620/18	Floppy Cat				36	36	36	38	48	70		60	67
5620/25	Floppy Cat				50	50	50	53	65	100		100	111
5625/18	Floppy Lamb				36	36	36	38	48	65		70	78
5625/25	Floppy Lamb				50	50	50	53	65	95		95	106
5651/16	Mini Floppy Bear										50	50	56
5652/16	Mini Floppy Polar Bear										50	50	56
5655/16	Mini Floppy Elephant										53	53	59
5658/16	Mini Floppy Rabbit										50	50	56
5662/16	Mini Floppy Dog										53	53	59
5665/16	Mini Floppy Cat										50	50	56
5668/16	Mini Floppy Lamb										50	50	56
5672/16	Mini Floppy Donkey										53	53	59
5675/16	Mini Floppy Pig										50	50	56
5678/16	Mini Floppy Fox										53	53	59
5700/20	Teddy	39	43	43								85	95
5700/30	Teddy	57	62	62								120	134
5701/22	Kiddi Bear										75	75	84
5702/20	Kiddi Bear										75	75	84

Steiff #	Description	1980-1981	1981-1982	1982-1983	1983-1984	1984-1985	1985-1986	1986	1987	1988	1989	1990	Current
5706/20	Kiddi Elephant										75	75	84
5710/20	Elephant	45										80	90
5710/30	Elephant	61	66									110	123
5712/20	Kiddi Dog										75	75	84
5715/20	Cocki	41	44	45								75	84
5715/30	Cocki	59	65									110	123
5717/20	Kiddi Cat										75	75	84
5717/20	Terrier	41	44									75	84
5717/30	Terrier	59	65									100	112
5720/20	Cat	39	43									69	77
5720/30	Cat	57	62									100	112
5722/20	Kiddi Mouse										75	75	84
5725/20	Floppy Lamb			41								75	84
5725/20	Kiddi Hedgehog										75	75	84
5725/30	Floppy Lamb			59								110	123
5728/20	Kiddi Fox										75	75	84
5750/22	Drolly Bear											52	58
5780/22	Drolly Cat											52	58
5790/22	Drolly Fox											52	58
5810/22	Elephant	43	48	49	49	49						79	88
5820/22	Dog	43	48									79	88
600393	Martini Bear, Polo, Ralph Lauren, NY, LE 1,500, 1994 U												800
6020/32	Poppy Raccoon										135	135	151
605884	Coal Christmas Ornament, LE 3500 U												165
6060/24	Poppy Rabbit, Blond										80	80	90
6060/32	Poppy Rabbit, Blond										130	130	146
6062/24	Poppy Rabbit, Cinnamon										80	52	58
6062/32	Poppy Rabbit, Cinnamon										130	83	92
606304	Steiff Watch, Charcoal, Teddy Baby, LE 4000												575
606502	Pendant Watch, Caramel, Teddy, LE 3000, 1993												500
6067/24	Poppy Rabbit, Grey										80	80	90
6067/32	Poppy Rabbit, Grey										130	130	146
6080/32	Poppy Cat										135	135	151
610158	(2) Steiff Bears plus Steiff Teddy Baren Book												750
6190/30	Chimp	38	47									75	84
6202/14	Friedericke, Yellow Goose									47	49	31	55
6203/26	Friedericke, Yellow Goose, Dressed Grl									80	85	85	95
6205/14	Frederic, White Gander									47	49	31	35
6206/26	Frederic, White Gander									80	85	85	95
6210/20	Cuddly Goose, Yellow										65	65	73
6210/32	Cuddly Goose, Yellow										100	100	112
6212/20	Cuddly Goose, Brown										65	65	73
6212/32	Cuddly Goose, Brown										100	100	112
6212/50	Cuddly Goose, Brown										200	200	224
6215/28	Possy Guenon Monkey										120	120	134
6215/30	Fox	40										72	81
6220/28	Possy Elephant										125	125	137
6225/28	Possy Cat										115	115	137
6228/28	Possy Lion										120	120	134
6235/30	Rabbit	40	40									70	78
6235/40	Rabbit	54	54									92	103
6240/20	Toldi Chimp			25	28							46	52
6240/28	Possy Fox										120	78	87
6240/30	Toldi Chimp			49	53							90	101
6242/20	Toldi Bear			25	28							48	54
6242/30	Toldi Bear			49	53	53						90	101
6245/28	Possy Hedgehog										115	115	129
6270/27	Toldi Bear									80		80	90
6271/27	Toldi Elephant									85		85	95
6272/27	Toldi Monkey									80		80	90
6273/27	Toldi Hedgehog									80	80	80	90
6274/27	Toldi Frog									80		80	90
6275/27	Toldi Cat									90		90	101
6276/27	Toldi Dog									80		80	90
6280/40	Dangling Rabbit		52									90	101
6280/70	Dangling Monkey											240	269

Steiff #	Description	1980-1981	1981-1982	1982-1983	1983-1984	1984-1985	1985-1986	1986	1987	1988	1989	1990	Current
6281/25	Lulac, Grey					43	43	46	57	80	83	55	62
6281/75	Lulac, Grey								200	300	300	195	218
6282/25	Lulac, Beige					43	43	46	57	80	83	55	62
6282/75	Lulac, Brown								200	300	300	300	336
6283/50	Lulac, Brown				72	72	72	76	92	130	135	86	151
6284/60	Dangling Dog	105	115									185	207
6284/99	Lulac, Cream										575	575	644
6285/55	Lulac Tiger			125	125	125	125					235	263
6285/60	Dangling Tomcat	105										185	207
6287/70	Dangling Dog											220	246
6288/32	Dangling Monkey "Mungo"							60	72			110	123
6290/32	Dangling Cat Burri							60	72	110		110	123
6291/32	Dangling Dog Lumpi							60	72	110		110	123
6292/32	Dangling Frog Cappy							60	72	110		110	123
6294/32	Dangling Mouse Pieps							60	72			110	123
6304/50	Hippo	170										300	336
6305/50	Rhino	170										300	336
6310/60	Bison	175	195	200	200	200						325	364
6314/60	Tiger	138	150	155	155							270	302
6315/30	Puma, Lying	75	75									145	162
6315/40	Puma, Standing	80	87									155	174
6315/99	Puma, Lying	375		425	425	425						750	840
6316/99	Puma, Sitting	590		700	700	700						1100	1232
6320/30	Leopard, Lying	75	82									145	162
6320/40	Leopard, Standing	80	80									155	174
6320/99	Leopard, Lying	375	415	425	425	425	425					750	840
6321/99	Leopard, Standing	590	650	675	675	675	675					1100	1499
6322/99	Leopard, Sitting St	695	713	700	700	700	700					1300	1456
6323/99	Panther, Lying	375	415	425	425	425						750	840
6325/99	Panther, Standing	590	650	675	675	675						1100	1232
6360/12	Teddy Shoulder Bag	10	11	12	12							22	25
6361/12	Teddy Coin Purse	10	11	12								22	25
6365/26	Teddy Shoulder Bag, Lg.	17	19	19	19							34	38
6370/22	Bear Music Box	49	54	54	54	54	54	54				97	109
6371/22	Cat Music Box	49										97	109
6376/18	Owl Music Box	44	48	49	49							88	99
6383/18	Ladybug Music Box	26	30									59	66
6400/15	Mosaic Ball, Sm., mhr	17	21	22								65	73
6400/20	Mosaic Ball, Med., mhr	28	32	32								110	123
6422/24	Donkey Pull Toy			62								115	129
6450/15	Ball				21	21	21	22	27	42		45	50
6450/20	Ball				32	32	32	34	41	65		69	77
6460/27	Chimpanzee (Hand Puppet)	26	28	28	28	28	28	30	36			50	56
6461/27	Bear (Hand Puppet)	26	28	28	28	28	28	30	36			60	67
6462/27	Frog (Hand Puppet)	26	28									50	56
6463/27	Rabbit (Hand Puppet)	30	33	33	33	33	33	35	42			55	62
6464/27	Dog (Hand Puppet)	30	32									55	62
6466/27	Cat (Hand Puppet)	30	33	33	33							55	62
6470/27	Owl (Hand Puppet)	30	33									55	62
6471/27	Lion (Hand Puppet)	33	36	37	37	37	37	39	47			62	69
6472/27	Fox (Hand Puppet)	33	36									62	69
6474/27	Wolf (Hand Puppet)	33	36									62	69
6476/27	Crocodile (Hand Puppet)	33	36									62	69
6485/32	Happy Bear										95	95	106
6488/32	Happy Guenon Monkey										105	105	118
6490/32	Happy Rabbit										105	105	118
6494/32	Happy Cat										115	115	129
6496/32	Happy Hedgehog										95	95	106
6497/32	Happy Fox										115	115	129
650529	Teddy Baby Ticket Seller, LE 5000, 1991 U												195
650550	Bear Back Rider Set, LE 5000, 1991 U												300
650574	Alice Teddy Bear, 40cm, LE 5000												325
650581	Wellington Bear, Polo, Ralph Lauren, NY, LE 1500, 1994 U												450
650581	Russia Bear, Polo, Ralph Lauren, NY, LE 1500, 1994 U												350

Steiff #	Description	1980-1981	1981-1982	1982-1983	1983-1984	1984-1985	1985-1986	1986	1987	1988	1989	1990	Current
650680	Harrods Musical Bear 1906, LE 2,000, 1993 **E**												400
650789	Louise Teddy Bear, 44cm, LE 3500												375
650819	Compass Rose Teddy Bear, 44cm, LE 3500 **U**												350
650901	Vedes Bear, LE 6000												350
650918	Orginal Teddy Bar 36, Spielzeug Ring, Baumwoll-sack, Germany, LE 3000 **W**												N/P
650925	Teddy Bar Eddi 27, Spiel & Spass, Baumwollsack, Germany, LE 2,000 **G**												N/P
651205	Teddy Donald, 30cm, WDW, LE 1500, 1993 **U**												550
651212	Teddy Donald, 60cm WDW, LE 25, 1993 **U**												3000
651243	Winnie the Pooh, WDW, LE 2500, 1994 **U**												700
651250	Winnie the Pooh, 60cm, WDW, LE 25, 1994 **U**												N/P
651270	Winnie the Pooh, 80cm, WDW, LE, 1994 **U**												N/P
651526	Teddy Bear, 30cm, Blond, DL, LE 1500, 1993 **U**												400
651533	Teddy Bear. 60cm, Blond, DL, LE 25, 1993 **U**												N/P
651540	Teddy Bear, 80cm, Blond, DL, LE 5, 1993 **U**												N/P
651847	Petsile, The Toy Store, LE 1000, 1993 **U**												195
651854	T.R., The Toy Store, LE 1,500, 1994 **U**												300
651861	Golli G & Teddi B, The Toy Store, LE 1500, 1995 **U**												400
651878	Molly Golli & Peg, The Toy Store, LE 2500, 1996 **U**												225
652080	Musikteddy 33, FAO Schwarz, LE 2000, 1993 **U**												350
6560/17	Teddy (Hand Puppet)											110	140
6600/17	Rabbit (Hand Puppet), mhr	20										85	95
6640/17	Fox Terrier (Hand Puppet), mhr	20										85	95
6660/17	Cat, Grey (Hand Puppet), mhr	20										85	95
6692/30	Bear (Hand Puppet)											85	95
6820/18	Lion (Hand Puppet), mhr	23										90	101
6880/17	Tiger (Hand Puppet), mhr	23										90	101
6991/30	Chimpanzee (Hand Puppet)	46	50	51	51	51	51	54	65			85	110
6992/30	Bear (Hand Puppet)	46	50	51	51	51	51	54	65			85	95
6993/30	Rabbit (Hand Puppet)	46	50	51	51	51	51	54	65			85	95
6994/30	Dog (Hand Puppet)	46	50									85	95
6995/30	Owl (Hand Puppet)	50	55									85	95
6996/30	Donkey (Hand Puppet)	46										85	95
6998/30	Cat	46	50									85	95
7010/45	Grey Jolly Rabbit Elbow Puppet									170		175	196
7086/10	Wool Bird Assmt	10	10									16	18
7116/08	Birds, Assmt	5	7	7	7							11	12
7136/04	Rabbits, Assmt	5	7	7	7	7						11	12
7146/06	Rabbits, Assmt	8	10	10	10	10	10	10	12			15	17
7156/08	Rabbits, Assmt	13	15	15	15	15	15	16	20			22	25
7170/06	Guniea Pig	9	9									15	17
7173/06	Hampster	8	8									12	13
7180/05	Frog	7	8	8	8							14	16
7180/07	Frog	8	10	10	10							16	18
7212/08	Duckling	9	10									14	16
7240/08	Rooster	7	8	8								11	12
7245/08	Rooster	9	11	11	11							16	18
7250/08	Hen	7	8	8								11	12
7255/08	Hen	9	11	11	11	11						16	18
7260/04	Chick	4	5	6	6							8	9
7260/06	Chick	5	7	7	7	7						10	11
7260/08	Chick	9	11	11	11							16	18
7276/09	Fish, Assmt	10	11									19	21
7354/04	Mouse, White	5	7	7	7							9	10
7355/04	Mouse, Grey	5	7	7	7							9	10
7370/03	Lady Bug	5	6	7								9	10
7370/04	Lady Bug	4	5	5	6							7	8
7370/06	Lady Bug	5	7	7	8							9	10
7390/10	Penquin	8	10									15	17
7480/06	Owl	7	9	9	9							12	13
7480/09	Owl	9	11	11	11							16	18
7492/05	Pitty Bear	6	7									15	17
7493/05	Pitty Fox	6	7									9	10
7494/05	Pitty Cat	6	7									9	10
7495/05	Pitty Rabbit	6	7			7	7	7				10	12

Key: W = World Wide • U = USA • E = England • G = Germany • WDW = Walt Disney World • DL = Disneyland • N/P = No prices available

NUMERICAL LISTING

Steiff #	Description	1980-1981	1981-1982	1982-1983	1983-1984	1984-1985	1985-1986	1986	1987	1988	1989	1990	Current
7496/05	Pitty Lamb	6	7									9	10
7497/05	Pitty Dog	6	7									9	10
7500/05	Pitty Elephant	6	7									9	10
7501/05	Pitty Lion	6	7									9	10
7502/05	Pitty Squirrel	6	7									9	10
7503/05	Pitty Mice	8	9									14	16
7580/27	Toldi Bear SOS										82	82	92
7627/12	Boy Mecki Character	13	16	17	18	20	20	21	27	45	45	45	50
7627/17	Man Mecki Character	32	39	39	41	50	50	53	65	95	95	95	106
7627/28	Man Mecki Character	410	60	61	65	70	70	75	90	145	145	145	162
7627/50	Mecki, Man			180	195	195	195					340	381
7628/12	Girl Mecki Character	13	16	17	18	20	20	21	27	45	45	45	50
7628/17	Woman Mecki Character	32	39	39	41	50	50	53	65	95	95	95	106
7628/28	Woman Mecki Character	410	60	61	65	70	70	75	90	145	145	145	162
7628/50	Mecki, Woman			180	195	195	195					340	381
7635/19	Santa Claus, LE 2000-1985							75	75	75		125	140
7635/28	Santa Claus, LE 1200-1984/2000-1985						95	95	100	100		155	174
7690/20	Shepard	31	34									60	67
7851/25	Doll, Madi			36								65	73
7860/20	Bambi Fawn					34	34	36				75	84
7871/28	Doll, Marion			43	43							80	90
7872/28	Doll, Marc			43	43							80	90
7873/28	Doll, Tanja			43	43							80	90
7874/28	Doll, Michael			43								80	90
7875/28	Doll, Yvonne			43								80	90
7892/40	Doll, Punch			56								100	112
8010/40	Riding Bear	185										355	398
8020/45	Rocking Duck	150										295	330
8130/50	Riding Animal, Rocking Bear			285	295	295	295	310	375	600	600	385	600
8135/50	Riding Animal, Rocking Pony			285	295	295	295	310	375	600	600	385	500
8150/40	Riding Animal, Riding Bear Rocker		205	210	215	285	285	300				395	442
8155/50	Riding Animal, Bear on Wheels		285	290	295							565	632
8175/60	Riding Animal, Pony on Wheels		295	300	300							570	638
8190/30	Riding Animal, Ladybug/Wheels		185	190	195	195	195	205	250	375		350	392
8195/45	Riding Animal, Rocking Duck		175	180	175	175	175					330	370
8452/22	Nimrod Bear, Caramel, Broken Set, LE					45						100	135
8453/22	Nimrod Bear, White, Broken Set, LE					45		35				96	135
8455/22	Nimrod Bear, Brass, Broken Set, LE					45						100	135
8470/17	Teeny Teddy Bag								60	77		80	90
8472/17	Teeny Bag Panda								60	55		60	67
8474/17	Teeny Bag Rabbit								60	55		60	67
8476/17	Teeny Bag Dog								60	55		60	67
8490/12	Teddy Minibag					12	12	12	15	22	22	23	25
8492/26	Teddy Bag					19	19	20	24	35		37	41
8494/03	Teddy Pin with Ribbon, mhr							20	19	19		22	25
8495/03	Teddy Pin, Beige, mhr					17	18	19	19			24	27
8496/03	Teddy Pin, Caramel, mhr					17	18	19	19			24	27
8497/03	Teddy Pin, White, mhr					17	18	19	19	19		24	27
8498/03	Teddy Pin, Chocolate, mhr					17	18	19	19	19		24	27
8500/03	Teddy Bear Pin					9	9	10	12	12		14	16
8501/02	Gold Plated Bar Pin w/Jointed Bear							15	18	27		22	25
8505/01	Gold Plated Teddy Earrings						20	21	27	46	46	46	52
8510/02	Gold Plated Teddy Necklace					15	15	16	20	32	32	210	33
8530/43	Steiff Watch, Blonde, Teddy Baby, LE 2000												675
8530/44	Steiff Watch, Brown, Teddy Baby, LE 2000, 1991												600
8550/02	Reg Edition, History of Steiff										100	100	112
8601/06	Porcelain Tea Set, 7 pc.								18	15		20	22
8605/01	Wall Plate										9	9	15
8605/06	Mini Tea Set										15	15	40
8605/15	Deluxe Tea Set										57	57	60
999079	Hercule Teddy, AMADE, Monaco, LE 3000, 1995												325
999765	Amelia, (with fliers coat/hat/goggles), I. Magnin, LE 650, 1993 U											600	
	Tinsel Christmas Ornament, LE 2500												195

ABOUT THE AUTHOR

Peter Consalvi, Sr. is a renowned toy industry sales representative and was associated with Reeves International, a distributor of Steiff bears and animals in the United States. Like all true collectors at heart, Peter remembers the initial spark in February 1970, that led to his becoming a Teddy Bear enthusiast. This was the year he attended his first New York Toy Show as a buyer for a unique hardware and toy store in Paoli, Pennsylvania. His only instructions were to buy what he liked and not be concerned with prices.

Consalvi recalls a feeling of awe sweeping over him when he entered the Reeves International Showroom filled with the most magnificent stuffed animals he had ever seen. A variety of bears ranging from large studio pieces to small animals were purchased that day.

"In the back of my mind I had hoped we had the clientele to resell these magnificent pieces. Not only did we sell them but we reordered every year!" exclaimed Consalvi.

After 11 years of selling retail, Consalvi was invited to join the firm of Gary & Riedel Co., which represented Reeves International. This position was to last for a short time as within two years, Consalvi was offered a position to represent Reeves directly. It was a position that he could not refuse and one that led him to an enjoyable and profitable 11 years selling Steiff bears and animals. Having represented Steiff at hundreds of shows, the author is amply qualified to comment and price the new popular American editions and museum collections.

OTHER STEIFF REFERENCE BOOKS

STEIFF SENSATIONAL TEDDY BEARS, ANIMALS & DOLLS
by Christel & Rolf Pistorius. Experience the endearing charm of Steiff's teddy bears and a bevy of animals in this richly illustrated, large format photograph album showcasing 100 years of the renowned German company. Certainly the most beguiling, colorful story of Steiff bears and animals, with 258 color photographs out of 288 photographs, ever published! 160 pages. 9" x 12-1/2". HB. Item #H3982. **$39.95**

4TH TEDDY BEAR & FRIENDS® PRICE GUIDE
by Linda Mullins. Latest values on bears, rabbits, cats and dogs as well as a wealth of other animals are featured! This book shows and values what is being collected today! Such important collectibles as Muffy, antique, collectible, manufacturer and artist are featured as well as a large section devoted to such popular companies as Steiff, North American Bear, Gund and limited editions from Steiff Museum Collection. Charts as well as 259 stunning b/w and 105 color photographs capture the character of bears and their friends. 192 pages. 6" x 9". PB. Item #H4438. **$12.95**